Tales from the Moon
Rosalia Moon Webster

Tales from the Moon
Rosalia Moon Webster

26
letter
PRESS

Big Sur, California
www.26letter.com

listen learn love

— Rosalia Moon

ISBN: 978-1-950731-04-6

Text by Rosalia Moon Webster
Cover Design byAnn Artz
Cover Illustration by Rosalia Moon Webster
Cover Photo by Brian Mack

Published by 26 Letter Press, Big Sur, California
www.26letter.com

For information about bulk purchases, sales, promotion, fund-raising, and educational needs -

Rosalia Webster - www.bigsurcus.com

This book is dedicated to Jessica Cooper, the Dancing Genie, the most enchanting belly dancer I know, to our life of artistry and friendship.

- *Rosalia Moon Webster*, BiG SuRCuS 2021

Contents

Foreward

Welcome to my poetry anthology. This is my collection of rap, requiems, spells, and musings. My creativity is a collage of mediums. I corralled my variety show of crafts into a toy box and named it BiG SuRCuS. In BiG SuRCuS, you will find poets, belly dancers, teachers, illustrators, herbalists, DJs, aerialists, fire dancers, youth, bohemians, wine professionals, millionaires, bubble blowers, lovers, families, outlaws, elders, friends, medicine women, mermaids, and many others. I am, at times, most of them. I write stories with this demiurgic cast, presenting ballyhoo and Prayerformance. We bring ceremony to our stages, teachings, actions, and thoughts.

Big Sur, a mesmerizing wealth of nature, has been my lifelong home. Mountains, forests, and sea are my habitat. Elements are my guide. Creatures and critters inspire my practice and habits. You will see and read my love of reverence, strength, sadness, moons, tides, wings, sundays, passion, and interesting characters.

The chakras of my tale are the title poems. This body of writing reflects my emotional journey, and intended influences. Poetic dance productions are created from my lyrics and performed with my troupe BiG SuRCuS. Shows are produced with my muse and Artistic Director, Jessica Cooper. I am indebted to the incredible family, patrons, artists, and fans, who together, throughout the decades, comprise BiG SuRCuS.

My purpose is to translate and preserve the peaceful and powerful energies of wilderness living. I strive to be kind and courteous, because the kids are always watching. I share my creative rites to help humans honor their part in positivity. My teachings and offerings from nature uplift and empower.

Each chapter contains work from a variety of years; I enjoy the perspective different ages and attitudes offer. I take liberties and any typing "errors" are intentional.

May this collection spark your goodness and stoke your passion. May I activate you to face our dystopian future, knowing your existence as a decent person matters.

In love and gratitude,

Rosalia Moon Webster 2021

Chapter 1. Toy Box
(Cabaret 2015)

I creatively blossomed in the absence of materialism. Abundance was provided by earth, not stores. I grew up with limited access to manufactured entertainment and amenities. I cultivated my expansion and education through imagination. I used reading, writing, drawing, and dancing, to create journeys. I was raised in a fairytale of my own making. No electricity ran through the mountains I called home. I read by lamplight. Washboards and clotheslines were romantic, yet necessary.

My mother raised chickens, made cookie bars, and baked bread. Mama Sara and Auntie Annette are the fourth generation of my family to live in their female-built Victorian in Pacific Grove. Auntie taught me to matchy matchy my outfits. Mama Sara taught me to celebrate life. We would camp and see concerts. We were dancing with folk from all over the globe.

Papa Ramon taught me sketching, carving, and art history in his cliff-side studio. He handed me novels to be read and told me to look up the words I did not understand. We played rhyming and spelling games. My isolated childhood was peppered with wanderers, crafters, traders, city folk, modern bards, and many family members, visiting our glorious homeland from around the world. I enjoyed desert summers with Papa Ramon's grandparents, Honey and Daddy Bye.

I am a fourth generation artist. At age three, my great grandfather carved for me my first wooden toy box. Great grandmother sewed cats, bunnies, and dolls, to fill my toy chest with friends. Tea was enjoyed with my conjured beings.

My great grandmother created stories and whispered them as I fell asleep. She stitched me clothes and bobby-pinned my cowlick. Honey taught me manners, respect, to be charitable, and the proper use of cutlery. My favorite utensil is the spoon. I am left-handed. I live in an antique-filled tree-house. I brew all these aspects in the cauldron of my artistry.

Toy Box speaks of the playfulness and joy which made me want to be curious.

The Alphabet of Directions, Elements, Herbs, and other useful words
Make your own poetic potion! - 2020

A is for Above, Aloe, Ancient, Autumn, and Ancestry

B is for Below, Borage, Black, Brave, Blue, Beast, and Beauty

C is for Chamomile, Comfort, and Comfrey
for Cozy, Cauldrons, Comet, and Courtesy

D is for Dandelion, Dream, Dare, Different, and Dance

E is for East, Earth, Echinacea, Elixir, and Elephant

F is for Fire, Fennel, Forest, Freedom, Future, Feather, and Fantastic

G is for Geranium, Ginger, Genie, Garden, Green, Glitter, Grape, and Gothic

H is for Herb, Hope, Hawk, Health, and Happiness

I is for Island, Idea, Ingest, Ingredient, and Interest

J is for Jasmine, Jade, Justice, Jungle, and Jazz

K is for Kelp, Knot, Kiss, Know, and Kindness

L is for Lavender, Lush, Love, Listen, and Laugh

M is for Mugwort, Metal, Mermaid, Music, Mountain, Moon, and Mask

N is for North, Nettle, Night, Nature, and Notion

O is for Oregano, Orange, Original, Outrageous, and Ocean

P is for Parsley, Poem, Purple, Planet, Potion, and Petal

Q is Quest, Quizzical, Queen, Quiet, and Quilt

R is for Rose, Rosemary, Remember, Respect, Red, and Rain

S is for South, Summer, Star, Spring, Smile, Sage, Scar, Sun, and Snake

T is for Thyme, Tea, Toy, Think, Thank, Twinkle, and Twirl

U is for Understand, Unguent, Unicorn, Universe, and Umbrella

V is for Violet, Velvet, Vision, and Vast

W is for West, Water, Wood, Willow, Winter, and Wilderness

X is for Xylophone, and the Roman Numeral Ten (X)

Y is for Yoga, Yerba, Yam, Yellow, and Yes

Z is for Zap, Zephyr, Zigzag, and Zeppelin
for Zero, Zip, Zest, Zeal, and Zen

Toy Box
2000

i grew up in a Toy Box
the one my great granddaddy carved for me
i grew up in a Toy Box
look at my friends smile at me
   most of them are make believe
and if they are real   they are sideshow freaks
i am laying my head down to sleep
   between crystal balls and dolls
      things with springs
         clowns and horns and bells   ring ring
and a Dancing Genie to make real my dreams
so you may see what great granddaddy made for me
i grew up in a Toy Box

BiG SuRCuS Life
2005

did you know we flew to your show in a UFO
did i mention we stepped through dimensions
we ride boulders down mountains
    lips to crystal creeks
we drink from cascading fountains
    strap on dirty boots
      for a moonlit hike
        frolic with feathers
          dance as we fly
we live in the   earth   fire   ocean   sky
we are blazing the trail to BiG SuRCuS life

Books
2020

from a lone childhood
into eternity   possibility
instruction   healing   sex   joy   grief
spun in paper pages
my friends were   bound   faded   stacked   dedicated

an air of importance about their shelf
entitled and titled unto themselves
i am everything due to stories
my great gram
whispered them as i fell asleep
    tales of conquest and glories
of morals and fables   she would speak

books bind our beliefs
    boast philosophies
they chart   science   wonder
    hopes and   dreams
in fragile stacks
stitched in delicate seams

resting in cobwebs   dust and dark
spines straighten when their pages part
their little letters begin to march
proudly spelling   tales of grit and heart

Danced Upon
2020

we are within this continuously transforming life
how exciting
the deep   elegant   heat   and   calm

before every dance i give thanks
for the invitation to sacrifice my moment upon the altar
how i honor the stages
i have   knelt   wept   and   lived   upon

Goodnight Pretty Queen
2001

good night until the sun does rise
sweet dreams my pretty queen
    until the dawn opens your eyes
and you bathe
    in morning sheen
yes sleep tight safe from harm
 for i your Noble Knight
watch your body as you sleep
    a temple in the night

(requiem for Pandi a black queen cat and Memorabilia
the tiniest calico)

Imagination
2015

imagination
live in a world created
    by courage and dreams

Joy In Birth
1995

alone for eternity
now
    representing humanity
        manifesting from galaxies

i stopped orbiting and fell from grace
    to abase my self on earth
i found joy in birth

My Three Desserts
1984

my first dessert was sweet potato
my second one was bread
my third dessert
was rice pudding
    then i went to bed

Nothing
2015

some great loves in my life
   are referred to as "Nothing"

this "No Thing' is my majesty
my temple   my throne
     sea and stone

Youth
2020

i never realized how young you were
now i ache
to appreciate
you
pretty momma

who used to wait so patiently
taking her time
spending her beauty

now i see
you are truly
younger than me

Regale Life
2020

do you regale life
illuminating your body with moonlight
inhaling comets and stars

when her heart breaks
do you hold the mountain
   letting her weep upon your shoulder

are you welcoming the trees
   their slow roots parading through earth

do you kiss the stone with your toes
as she bounces down the hill
   somersaults into the path

do you ask the birds how they sing such   divinity
do you regale life

Relations
2015

to all my relations
who walk the road
         before me
this dance is for you

soft step is my prayer
breath is my flight
every day i hold you in my heart

Time To Play
2003

tick tock we are tied to the clock
 bag of bones with mechanical thoughts
dance of the drone   until we drop
we work
      and we work
           and we never stop
it is hard to explain the tick trap in our brain
we sweat for a pleasure that is never gained
work is worth   the illusion bought
our soul is caught
we gear to win
springs coiled tight within
let us cast the hands of time away
seconds
   minutes
     hours
      days
give us strength to be free to play
give us freedom to be strong to pray
tic tock strong to pray

Chapter 2. West of Eden
(Cabaret 2016)

As a pioneer woman in the time of technology I forged a unique identity. When the world was in industrial revolution, our wandering coastal highway was just being dynamite-blasted into limestone cliffs. I live in the land of wildfires. Our community is often isolated up to a year or more due to mudslides. Being raised country meant moon-circles, night-swims, bonfires, potlucks, and bookmobiles.

I have never used a gym. I cultivate my dance, yoga and strength in the great outdoors. My physical youth was a kaleidoscope of chopping wood to cook or heat my tub and digging in the garden with Mama Sara. I rode towering waves, drove dirt roads, and hiked golden hills. I choose to mirror the grit and grace of this land.

Mountain lions roam. Foxes ask. Butterflies flutter. Hummingbirds sip nectar. Condors return. Hawks and eagles soar. Whales breach. There is a physical and spiritual reward for opting to clamber landslides, twisted roots, and beaches. It is under the vast sky, kissed with sea mist, where I download my ideas. There is a solemnity in me desiring months without interaction with an urban world.

I met the Rinpoche at a teacher's Buddhist temple. I learned circus with Wavy Gravy. I studied African Dance with Baba Olatunji. Aprendí español en la playa. I learned fire dance from an auntie. I practiced yoga in Costa Rica.

My education is extremely different from metropolitan schooling. I find my perspective is applicable even in these science fiction times, and may be refreshing and enlightening to others. There is still a place for an avant-garde in a civic sphere. My inimitable life exists due to souls I will never meet in person. I praise and represent them through my art. My ancestors came from the fairylands of Scotland, traveling over seas and down the Oregon Trail.

My foremothers came in canoes from South America, and up through the Yucatan, into Arizona, and on to California. Two worlds met. I was born. My eyes are emerald green, my skin the hue of golden coins. With so few people around, I befriended all ages and learned from everyone. I did not understand my differences until much later. Now, I toss comfort to the wind in exchange for life on this frontier. In gratitude, West Of Eden is an ode to those who got me here.

Tales from the Moon

Composed
2016

composed
of spirit   heart   and bone
we bring it on home
to the land where we were grown
in this day and age   the earth is paved
                                        elements rage
BiG SuRCuS conjures   prayer   potion   and play
honoring rugged lands over surreal coasts
infinite years ago
sacred clowns came dancing in
ladies   they   them   and gentlemen
welcome to the West Of Eden

Bones
2016

we are one body
　your sand and stones are my bones
　　honor and love us

Broken Day
2013

day break peacefully apart
porcelain window heart
                                   not shattered

grey gentle
wings of swan
        song of dawns
spill forth
  light
            gush
                    love
adore

sun
  lazily rise
      your smile
opens life

Country Girl version I
2000

raise hearts and hands
thank the goddess for the land
when we breathe
bow down to the trees

when a bird flies
hi to the skies
        hello father hawk
listen when wise owl talks
sylvan secrets the forest shares
we are aware
    our lair is rich
our generation   our nation of the mountains
is a fountain overflowing
jade   gems   feathers
      earthen treasure
           she does give
so we may naturally   lavishly live
   suns   moons   milky ways
          and stars

her fortune is ours
so we take charge
we represent her
    we present her to you
      we ask that you love this land
like we country girls do

Eagle
2016

> live in the great now
>   soar with the eagle
> present   this sacred moment

Earth Made Me
1995

> bare feet on stone
> sweet pungent air
>   eternal aum
> actions of care
>
> powerful mountains
> high places of energy
>   i am simply
> the way earth made me

Embrace The Day
2015

> embrace the day
> blow your mind away
>   radiate
> glorious morning
>   she awakes

Country Girl version II
2000

like mountain streams
our rap is flowing free
befriending time
   growing deep
traveling through history
deep and rootsy
               like an old oak tree
creating   connectivity   family
   honoring

Flow
2020

morning flow
vision soft and sharp
   through portals

Future Country Girls
2002

future country girls speak poetry
   tales of galaxies and old oak trees
praise the planets and peaks we cross
 sweet our talk   dirty our walk
swill milky way   eat homemade
swim through time and mermaid caves
golden hearts   eyes of jade
we see and love   new worlds and ways
health   happiness   beauty   and grace
honor earth and outer space

 rocket to my world
 let freedom ring
future country girls
drink moonbeams
galactic dreams
        all we want it seems
   future country girls

Gem
2020

disappear
ghost   mist   diamond
i am a sparkle in the eye of eternity
i am a giggle in the laughter of infinity
my fleeting star almost instantaneously
                              feeds the bonfires of forever
my insignificance magnificent
                           connectivity to the
cosmic fabric

Hail These Females
2001

hail these females
we scratch laws with claws
hunt the false
 lead the lost
      we march strong
with rhythm in our blood
     hope in our song
with my pride at my back
my crew in a pack
we attack
    sadness
       badness
        madness
the type of stuff that we have had enough of
until all transforms
sunshine in a storm
until we are warm
by peace to the core
     my roar
        my prayer
is a chant in the air
that we will
    rise
      thrive
        survive
          and stand
throw high our hands
give thanks for the land

Hawk
2008

soar   fierce
pierce
   like arrows
       the wind

wings
bring speed
  eyes hunt

warriors
of the air
ancient

mighty

lover
of life
grace my
  vision

Lady Rose
1998

i'm Lady Rose the thorny part of the pack
my girls blush at how silly i act
i play with my words with fire in my hand
  roses grow sweeter in rugged lands

when the rain falls   i splash in puddles
when the mountains crumble   i dance in rubble
i calm the trouble   i study the fumble
this lioness is rough and tumble

around the world many friends i have made
lovely liaisons with outer space
roll the red out   over the paved
because queens rule the kingdom today

Land Is Queen
2001

regal world
nature is our mother
we are guardians of her treasure
we delight in natural pleasure
play in her domain
honor the land
she is Queen

Lay Down
2008

call across your kingdom
   ring words
  echo commands
march your minions
        succeed and stand
fall with your freedom
impaled with truth
    conquerors die
the land reaps all youth

Lyrical
2016

      wilderness music
   song of ocean and mountain
         awake rejoice dance

Mother Sky
2018

why does your beauty fill me
completely wholly
   Holy

Mountains
2016

strength mountain
compassion ocean
dance wind

Path
2014

dance laugh splash
aum chant rejoice bask
sun sea land path

Praise
2015

spirit awake
   ring the day
         be free
pass away
     praise the grace
        of eternity

Rain Fire
2020

rain and flame
cleanse   anoint   rebirth
baptism

Rainfire
2020

heated storm   evaporate my fear
swords of rain kill insecurities
mighty royal solitude
        enthrone me upon   stone shores

awakening
            to our story

Rocky Road
1997

dancing path   is our home
beauty the unknown turn
honor   the unturned stone

relations alive in us
walk our blessings
    upon   our rocky roads

The Burn
2006

do you
 feel it
  crave it
know   its presence

are you afraid of the burn
timid to turn
         and face desire

fire may nourish
     the phoenix flame
you are love anyway
  even alone

Eden of The West
2015

born of those   who braved this coast
over land and sea   heeding mystery
lions cave
     hawk nest
respect   strength   breath
life within wilderness
   Eden of The West

Chapter 3. Limelight
(Cabaret 2018)

The stage is a place to share ideals and convictions. Here I offer lessons from my own experiences. This comedy and tragedy theatre allows me to be both fierce and lightly entertaining. I believe in human decency and common courtesy. I have no stomach for cruelty. I am inspired by love. I was fifteen when I first lived alone and supported myself. I've owned my own businesses since I was eighteen. BiG SuRCuS has been my canvas for over twenty years. I offer my multidimensional forum as a compass to navigate the wonder, sorrow, and bliss of life. I help bright and curious minds connect.

Art is essence and essential, frivolous and defiant. With BiG SuRCuS, we create original and profound pieces. We explore creative friendships, build spectaculars, express story, and produce personal prose. We flex our ability to demonstrate, and stand for those unable. We teach by example. Here in our world of dress-up and fables, we create light so others may shine. We make space, so others may

grow. We are bold and daring so others may find their con-
fidence. This chapter showcases how we share our philoso-
phy and Prayerformance under the BiG SuRCuS limelight.

Tales from the Moon

Limelight
2018

love in the limelight
we are all made of stars
empress   diva   sage
circle   altar   stage
honor   strength   and heart

language of light
dance   prayer   and though
paint in caves   conjure   create
translate   activating art

casting our spotlight
balance brilliance and dark
illuminate truth
walk the path of the moon
cosmic fabric we all are

BiG SuRCuS shines   golden times
in dystopian minds
dancers   Dakini   and me
weave love for you eternally
under the limelight

Poem for Dakini
2018

all alone in the trees
i wish i had a friend
not just make-believe
like the one in my head
and if i did
she would look like this

hair made of sky
eyes made of stars
light in her laugh
joy beats her heart
she has dance in her walk
music in her depths
her tears are crystal dolphins
her dress is spider web

she will be my friend
my Dancing Genie   Dream Dakini
feathers in hand
dripping jewels from her lips
creating legends with the sway of her sensuous hips

scrying divine truth with her fingertips
all the tales i write
she does brings to life
now i have a friend to share the limelight

(for Jessica Cooper my Dancing Genie)

Moon Rider
2015

are you a moon-rider
harnessing the mighty orb
                          of gold and shadow

do you dream of the beast   during the day
as she sleeps   beneath the blanket of light
 do you wonder   is she rested
to once more carry you through the night

are you a moon-rider

Moon Path
2020

this time   is the dawn of eternity
this dance   is my first   and last
this moment did not exist   and will echo into forever
i do not cling to memories
i let them wash me   tides on shores
 tears on skin
moon paths on water

Pages
2001

my words crave
      pages of passion

longing
to sweet whisper in your ear

my dances
  desire
      to linger
caresses
  on your
    tender
      skin dear

Self
2016

reflection of dreams
mirrors of moons   stars   and self
we are creators

The Way
2016

act upon the truth
with your breath   thought   and movement
the way of the dance

Ghost
2020

how fun to receive a sash of sister-hood
        across the web of time
                from her dream to mine
oh the stories this   SILK   will see
 fingers have sewn and will caress it
    smiles it will evoke
        tears it will catch
        scars it will swath   souls it will send
 you will have always witnessed her first dance
and you will be there when she takes the stage
                                again
who is she   this ghost of dancing black
what is her name

Silk
2020

silk portal
  sweet dancing moon tears
    spirit veil

Spring
2016

live last day of spring
water-dreams believe blossom
come harvest summer

Spun
1999

                spun
          strung
        stung
  run through
   gutted

my remorse echoes into hollow cavities
which should be you

Sunday
2020

there was never a beginning   or end
there was always sunday
calling me   kissing my eyelids
a   three-hour-brunch
this gentle day hugs me under down
this sweet day says rest   sing
everything is potential   all is well
the   weeks   months   eons
                are a kaleidoscope   pattern
      a cauldron of magic   all bubbly and brilliant
together
yet sunday says here i am in a dressing gown
  here i whisper sweet nothings
those other days request productivity and abandonment
  i am here to brew your tea   restore your power
hold your heart   brush your tear   and renew your joy
    I am sunday

Storm
2020

eye of the storm
  silent vacuum
  brightest black   cocoon
rest angel
      fall through heaven
           breathe

Understand
2000

let us try to understand
each other
             take steps
  move forward
together

Veils
2020

cross over   the veil
           we will write tales of your dance
send our love   with you

Venus Songs
2020

 pumping blood
dusty sunbeams of love
black holds the rainbow
the careless thoughtful greedy giving
 scared brave
 feared wronged
 my heart beats for you
singing venus songs

Workshop
2018

cast aside   ties and binds
      my city sideshow
         and frolic free
i invite you
allow me to conjure   and write you
into my tales
and fantasies
  let us visit ancient underworlds
   and divine   timeless   realms
         as healers and gentle beings
downloading   coding   and receiving
weave friends weave
into my imagination
become my stories

Chapter 4. Beautymark
(Cabaret 2019)

Proclaiming my peculiarities became my beauty. Life is both revelry and a rite of passage. I welcome the brilliant and bizarre.

This chapter is a tip of the hat to every time I queried -- what if I turn it upside-down, what if I wear a mustache, what if I stand up for them, what if I do it my way? My art is a rejoicing for each time I dare to speak my mind, dress extravagantly, perform in front of thousands of people, stay home, am quiet, am alone. It was a tremendous night when I finally realized I must embrace my personal story. I was to celebrate my one-of-a-kind success. (So said the imaginary parade of elephants, can-can dancers, and circus dolls creating ballyhoo behind me that fateful evening.)

I have been regal and poised. I have abased myself. I have fallen madly in love and broken my heart. I have held the dying and newborn in my embrace. I am akin to the mythical phoenix bird, I burn and rise in brilliance.

BiG SuRCuS is a stage I built for all, those who struggle, seek, who support, or need to be lifted. I hold court for vagabonds and queens marching to their own drum. I have space for the artist, hermit, spiritual, wounded, recluse, lover, assaulted, alchemist, and warrior. Praise to those who find a voice and those we speak for. This is a tribute to those I champion. Beautymark hails the power of being a fantastical child, and how our curiosities become our confidences.

Beautymark
2019

confident curiosities
you swoon at our oddities
we were born these strange beauties
with elegant eccentricities

we are brave   brilliant   and bizarre
sensational   sideshow freaks
casting shadows   showing scars
bejeweled tears over blushing cheeks

born paupers   queens   or in-between
we are sirens singing SuRCuS song
revealing masked magnificence
we are the stunning   weak and strong

true comedy and tragedy
stories of   life   strife   romance
dreamt and birthed beneath limelight
exhibit   extraordinary dance

pumping in the dark corporeal
grotesque and gorgeous beats our heart
while angels and demons hail
our beast becomes   our Beauty Mark

Cat Likes To Rap
1999

middle of the day take a nap
while girls purr and flap
   curl in a verbal-lap
their cunning quotes evoke   dream-laughs
tongue-rhymes   wash over like a bath
warmth and words wrap this cat
this cat likes the rap

meow and purr on the mic
live nine lives
see at night
velvet fur   silky strides
power of the verbalized

chanting charms
casting spells
cat nip songs
 in the blue-bird day
vintage jazz is on
this cat is napping in
 golden sun
this cat likes to rap

Wound
2020

missing you
is the greatest ache

     a loved wound

Dark Night
2001

come play for a while

     please don't stay
come with me
come with me

i will take you to the sky
take you to be high
  fear i hide
my truth wrapped in lies

i will be the light side of your dark night
the light side of your dark night

Black Friday
2013

grab

        stab her in the back
machines march   shadows cast
a last grin   upon her lips
burst of life   before the slip

in commerce she had drown
another mother crushed her down
fighting more as dreams grew
for all she desired as a youth

tooth and nail so child would not lack
yet in vain she died on Friday black

Denial
1998

do i choose to lose
struggle to be   brought down
defender of denial
my peachy heart
               bruised
forgoing ceremony
  steeped in trial

First Of December
2013

year was young
           spring sprung
now
  gradient grays
  fade this way

hold fast
  month last   first day
  pearl in sand
your end grand
your bow grace

Fleeting Love
2020

it was an achingly beautiful dance   solemn and chilled
just a sip in her cup   yet she shared
                      her love beside her
          she smiled on me
it was a dance that tore at my soul
and filled me with an emptiness to be explored
darkness to be illuminated

Talons
2016

no more
to pour forth
passion
with a lion roar
           now frozen tundra

wrestle lighting and thunder
to ensure your comfort
   see you tender

fierce with claws
screeching and raw
  my talons
       are only truly sharp
to protect me as i set you free
go live your waves   your edge   your wings

Beast
2020

you   dark   beast
truth familiar
within me

Hold Your Heart
2016

i hold your heart dear
sunshine rushes in our blood
you our earth mother

Kinky Kat
1999

she always
watches in a silky
stealth way
Kinky Kat
she always
wishes
to be
watched

Kiss
1998

i want a real kiss
on the lips
roll my hips
let the tongue slip
fingers grip
your hair

stare
into your eyes
you look wild
i smile
snap back
your head
expose your neck
i'll soon be fed

i want a kiss
hungry
eating me
biting
exciting
igniting
lightning shot
hot
locked
caught
sought
naughty and haughty
i crave a lot
i want a kiss   real enough to want

Leave
1998

look at me
      i leave to please

and squeeze my eyes
      in fear
     my tears
will never dry

Sunday Storm
2020

          dark sunday
skywater falling
  hidden rays

Sunday
2020

this sunday
find peace and balance
calm the storm

Reveal
2020

afraid to reveal
unmask spirit soul and dream
essence always seen

Self Centered
2014

i am so self-centered   the world revolves around me
i am so self-centered   it is me i'm trying to please
i cannot meet your needs
     i cannot hear your pleas
  or see you on your knees
       because i am so focused on me
i am so self-centered
        it is the loneliest place to be

Succulent Racy
1997

pretty fine
    succulent mine
for tonight
  i writhe
     caught tangled in a rough touch
lady lover
   never stay over
just play with pleasure

Sleep
2015

dreams on wings flutter
   webs of dimensions travelled
        nighttime adventures

Watching
2008

she is watching
    wanting him

it is sin
   to not show
   let him know
before he goes

that his
   kiss
   bliss
thrills her
forever

Wholly Holy
2020

my temple
this holy wholeness
aloneness
plump   ripe   bursting
                              solitude
i could not speak to you
    of this   from here
       my realm of quiet
where i am long   longing to be

there was a time of unity
                         never met
a queen captured
                      in make believe
dreams of communion
seeking mana   bread and wine
had by many hands   not mine
there was a time of togetherness
       left
me breaking   weeping

now in my shadow moon temple
no longer the fool
            no blame or shame
i cleared my dna
 forgiveness and comfort for those who precede
not after
i will bear no fruit
    have shed my leaves
i will not harvest myself into future beings
          i am   my eternity
my forever belonging only to me
        singular divinity

i find the path, the thread again and again
weaving patterns only i understand
rediscovering the journey
each breath   each step
i forge into the great mystery
            becoming becoming   wholly holy

Fairies
2001

be kissed in the mist
with berries brought by fairies
      they place in your lips
               wash down with tea of rosehips

Sky Castle
1998

do not say goodbye

wait for me

                        eternally

in the castle in the sky

The Art of Being Alone
2020

meditate
    or recreate memories
    you are truly free
  when you stand solo
in eternity
   spend days   taking time to breathe
not longing to see
          or desiring to need
    the time for poetry
for getting to know your "Me"
  wind befriends your skin
     sun soaks in
 seas crash your dreams
 imaginings become reality

there is beauty in your silent laugh
your stone strewn path
           cause in your
           solitude
your quiet is a jewel
that has no company
no two or three
there is only your most divine "Me"

Chapter 5. Caravana Alquemia (Cabaret 2020)

Lessons provided by the sylvan wild helped me mature into a conscious, considerate being. Nature's harmony coaxed and converted growth from pain, hope from loss, and celebration from brokenness.

In the country, I rise with the sun and eat seasonal harvest. I cultivate local sages for wands and potions. I adventure with the tide. I build muscle, and deepen my spirituality, by climbing, scrambling, and roaming the altars formed by our planet. I have welcomed and sung farewell to many souls. My friendships extend to those no longer here on earth. I find peace knowing that I, too, will make the sacred journey of leaving life. My womanly body is tuned to the moon. I wear gems from the beaches, and feathers from the sky.

My medicine tools are the woods I wander and sunsets I behold. The land I coexist with adorns and anoints me. The fairy fjords and jungle temples of my ancestors resonate in my good work. From the Dance Temple perch I watch an artist studio crumble, slowly returning to the sea. It is the house of late Edmund Kara, my papa's carving mentor. The decaying, creeping studio is an homage, an offering upon the shrine. Our workshops are holy places. I conduct remembrances, rites, alchemy, and initiations. I lead altar building, fire safety, and poetry immersions. From my home, I have brought my Prayerformance and fire-dance to world festivals, ancient sites, and tropical lands.

Big Sur is my elemental mandala. This chapter is a bow to the teachings I channel from the beyond. Caravana Alquemia is the timeless magical parade we are travelling in together.

Caravana Alquemia
2015

mi llama Rosalia
hoy caravana alquemia
y cuando luna esta nueva
con fuego brujas bailas
i am Rosalia
this is caravana alquemia
under starry skies
let us dance with light
our auric medicine
illuminates the circle
blooming a surreal
BiG SuRCuS ritual
we gather   we remember
barefoot with two feathers
   conjure elementi
      following the signs
         siga el presagio
            cosmos space and time
we are the fabric of creation
there is no end to life

mi llama Rosalia
con ballerinas y Jessica
circo grande alquemia

Alight
2016

alight my shores love
i am the sea calling you
　　my wave is your home

Anew
2016

　　　crawling from morning
　born anew in each moment
the mother and child

Between
2020

how was it
　the light between dark
　　　　　known as day

Cloak
2004

cloaked in couture spirituality
　in line
　　to be defined

or
DECLINE

create conscious mind
　connectivity

　　　why sell and buy
the sacred and divine

Crescent Moon
2020

crescent moon
chalice   holy grail   vessel   heart
 guide our rivers of lifeblood
                              call forth seed and tide
 empress in the sky

Dancing Moon
2020

were you there
 dancing with the moon
and venus

Death
1995

it holds her hand as she dips into the wet
then brings her up for a breath
        saying to death
not yet

Existing
2020

elements
    always becoming
  existing

Give Praise
2004

give praise
>lay upon the altar
>>be ceremony
>>ancient electric
new beginnings
olden ways
we are forever

Grey Wing
2015

stark skies churn   bruised clouds
thoughts fly   seagulls on grey wing
>moody happiness

Harmonize
2020

living within the outdoors is necessary
>My "self"
is synchronized with nature

wilderness soul

what fun frolicking forest
>breeze lift my cape   my heart
spirit harmonize   with cosmic song

Ibis
2015

ocean fog
majestic dawn
      mighty ibis
stand strong

grand wing
feather drum
carry prayer
fly home

(for Grandpa Ralph 1934-2015)

Keepers
2020

we are all walking her trails
of veins lava river mud stone and sea
she called us here
                as her mothers and keepers

are we standing by her side   under her wing
    at the vanguard

is this light beauty strangeness and strength
                                    her sword
are we warriors protecting her flank

stand strong
            for the weak   the meek
                each other
                earth mother

Little Moon
2020

spiral moon
   waxing in her crest

sipping souls

Poison
1990

poison daggers through me
   the love i kindled for you
      a serum

metamorphosis of hot tears
      liquid lost hope
love dies

Pretend
1999

alone i lie after dark
what about light can i trust
from the night my daydreams run
i really don't care if morning comes
the sky is nice so dark above
i'd rather be lonely
   than pretend to love

Real
2020

consort with reality before she consumes
desire   creativity   hope

look her in the eye
seek beauty in her darkness
   a path through madness
           peace in her fury

Rise
2015

rise golden feather
  breathing your eternity
    grace the mighty sky

Silent is the Smoke
1987

silent is the smoke
sacred is the prayer
message whispered in our hearts
becomes a spirit
  of the air
our blessings are delivered
although few words are spoke
prayers travel to the spirit
in   circle   dance   and smoke

(for Uncle Markie 1957-1986)

This Now
2010

come to me love
  share joy
    caress of skin
      shiver of song   and tenderness

before i am gone
and this now we hold ends

for i will die
  and become the moon and sky
    sea and galaxy
  i will be the wind
sit with me now
while i am your love   your friend

Weep
2016

reach deep the earth weeps
ripping out her heart   she bleeds
    love seeps   bloody beats

Welcome
1990

am i going to die

  not today my love

he closed his eyes
took his last earthly breath
    i kissed him goodbye
whispered
welcome to eternal life

Wind
2020

caressing
silken breath of sky
wild free wind

End Of The Road
2015

approaching the end of the road
i feel my knowing go
my choices grow

if time stood still or froze
death would not pause from being close

breath beginning to slow

even with love that freely flows
          from me to you   you to me
    life i leave
to embrace eternity

Princess Moon
1998

princess alone   on her throne
    cast stones
from castle cracks

  only the moon
    brave as her heart
      shines to sea a path
    shadows hold her hand
this evening   this breath her last

Requiem
2020

you are missed
sons of wilderness
                darkened light

Requiem
2020

there is a wild in this coast
A spiral of high and deep
of valleys and peaks   of falls and creeks
there is a circle of drums
secrets   spirits   angels
there is a time we
                welcome and farewell

every turn you reach   we love you
when you fly away home   we sing you there

(requiem for those Big Sur souls flying young)

Chapter 6. Cauldron
(Cabaret 2021)

This is my Happily Ever After and Once Upon A Time. It is
the beginning of the year. I have already navigated a flash
flood, written poems, hunted for jade, taught dance, taken
classes, and frolicked under the moon. I have harvested
mandarins and hibiscus and patience and understanding.
And I'm continuing the tales I have spun for you. Please
reach out for the BiG SuRCuS experience in real time. We
have learned so much together. We know each moment
of happiness is earned. We know to help others in their
quest for safety. We will navigate towards peace. We have
overcome judgments and labels. Our senses are alert. Our
gestures, words, and thoughts are considerate. We are clean-
ing up the over-spilling porridge pot of wants and demands
flowing towards us from so many directions. Let us live in
right relationship with the Earth. Be Healthy Sexy and Put
The Lid On Your Cauldron. With love,
 Rosalia Moon Webster

Cauldron
2021

mental alchemy
think act and be
our gold is passion and philosophy

 bare-bones or bounty
less or plenty
 a nest of needs are we
 guide our energy fit lock and key
 before we   cast or quest   prepare wisely

 harness conceits   vex vanities
 satisfy
 responsibly
render harmony
from gothic tapestry

opulence is a shared cup of tea
equality for all
 common courtesy
 ritual is the act of caring
the will to listen   learn   love   and lead

brains think   minds free   hearts beat
 synapsis firing
 page to pen   mic to mouth   stage to feet
mantras of earth-core
we are death   birth and   life force

cast runes   read cards   symbols   signs   and stars
our alphabets   glyphs   and carving tablets
   create fables   fates   and lore
to fortify our psychic shore

blow candles dark   let directions release
thank the elements for their serving
   brooms sweep sweep
 bathe in sea and moon beams
wash with gratitude so reverence gleams

unplug for cerebral clarity
 stimulate the pink activate qi
stow tools come dawn
when rites are done
veils are drawn   we put the lid on our cauldron

Raise Your Glass Again
2021

when you cross the rainbow bridge
turn and raise your glass again

connection flows like wine
across seas and over time
tales of the vine
friendship aged harmoniously
the structure the bouquet
the wood and yeast

love by the glass   magnum   jeroboam
nighst grew shorter   comradery grew long
balanced blend of styles and smiles farmers and somms

for long ago in fields of stone
on a barren field
shore of loam
cliff of limestone
in Burgundy   Champagne   Barossa   or Rhone
when that first grape was grown
celebration found a home

this colorful family of mothers   artists   and athletes
but mainly wine geeks
lending an ear to hear
a heart to care
 a shoulder on which to lean
pull together in a time like this
we have lost a brother celebrated and missed

we share his capers and memories
recall his charm his glories
toasting his purple suit and legacy
hip hip hooray for him
good ol jim
when you cross that rainbow bridge turn and say
cheers my friends
and raise your glass again

Lasers and Sages
2020

BiG SuRCuS is shy   coy   and outrageous
from stone to dystopian ages
    we clear your light year with lasers and sages

free of the virtual cage
clear of mindless craves
soap box to stage
we play   we pray   we demonstrate

our practice   potions   and tisanes
keep us safely strange
    creatively insane
growing horns   spreading wings
we are nightmares   fairytales   laughs   and screams

dwelling on shores   near creeks   in caves
marvelously mannered
kissed with dusty grace
    connecting within the contemporary maze
we program our infinite ancient ways

subliminal courses for minds to eat and eat
 to feed   a hole   a goal   a need
some feast on illusions
we rsvp   a more fulfilling recipe
we see the soul in everything

we view buildings as trees
automaton critters clack and beep
upon glass leaves
   into steel and concrete
     we weave wild majesty

circuits ache break or quake near me
 electricity acts unique
communicating with my fleshy being
i make friends with the machines
we dance with technology

life is the place we perceive
 a matrix desires a stroll by a stream
 man-made realities have goddess dreams
  BiG SuRCuS stands up to be Healthy-Sexy and free

SIREN SONG
2021

from caverns we swim   slip into life
let us comfort conscious   ebb mental tides
we are in your psyche slaking primal need
savoring the salt of joy of grief

counters of trust   treasure   curses   and cures
watchers of wisdom   wagers   and wars
we play fair seek balance   and welcome peace
forgoing fight to love fearlessly

we dry the tears of your sadness darling
dance and rejoice while we soothe your mourning
sip our lullabies   for your peaceful sleep
your secrets   desires   and wishes we keep

we are choice   chance   fangs   fins   and shipwrecks
naiad mirage of hope   success   and lament
crashing into thoughts on cranial shores
moral compass worn   scales scarred our tails torn

you may emerge from this mer-mind dive
return to sanity   land and moonlight
yet veins will pulse a new wondrous thrum
 for your heart now sings the siren song

I am a pioneer, poet, leo, lover, dancer, medicine woman, living a friend filled, well read, well traveled, epicurean, circus, life.

Thank you for opening this book. Thank you for supporting my art.

I am grateful for poets who have inspired me:
Anais Nin
Rumi
Kahlil Gibran
Missy Elliot
e.e. cummings

Made in the USA
Columbia, SC
02 September 2021

A Mystical Path Less Traveled:
A Jungian Psychological Perspective

It took real courage to write this book, in which we are led on a journey to let go of our 'old time religions,' in order to directly experience the numinosity of everyday life. Jung called upon each of us to connect to the infinite and Jerry's book helps us do just that. I am deeply appreciative for this spiritual gift.

- **Jeffery T. Kiehl, Ph.D.**, Jungian Analyst, author of *Facing Climate Change: An Integrated Path to the Future.*

Here Jerry R. Wright has woven together poems, personal journal entries, and informative psychological perspectives to show how a mystical pathway of encounter with the numinous is available to all – believer and nonbeliever alike – through the human psyche. These evocative pages will certainly encourage those with "a hunger for the holy" to join Jerry in this delicious banquet. Here we are invited to embrace a mature and authentic spirituality that acknowledges our capacities for both creation and destruction while honoring the divine mysteries deep within us, and in the larger world. The blessings written for Iona pilgrims alone are worth the price of admission. A beautiful read!

- **Sheri D. Kling, Ph.D.**, author of *A Process Spirituality: Christian and Transreligious Resources for Transformation* and founder of DeeperRhythm.net.

In describing A Mystical Path Less Traveled I will steal shamelessly from the author because it is hard to improve upon his own words. The book is "directed to those who have a hunger for the holy," and readers who fit that description will devour this book. In the sharing of journal entries, poems, blessings, and dreams,

Jerry Wright opens his personal backpack filled with "both angels and monsters" and gives us a look at the outer world and inner world through his very perceptive eyes. This honest, sometimes gut wrenching, often humorous book sent "chills up my spine / And down to the soles of my feet."

- **Alice Smith**, author of several collections of poetry including *That Little Girl* and *Reimagining*.

Carl Rodgers wrote: "That which is most personal is most universal." Dr. Wright in this psycho/spiritual worldview - A Mystical Path Less Traveled - *provides a resource for all searchers on a spiritual path. With reflections on journal entries, poems, dreams, and blessings, he provides an excellent resource for those who seek meaning and purpose.*

- **J. Pittman McGehee, D.D.**, Episcopal Priest, Jungian Analyst, author of seven books.

A MYSTICAL PATH LESS TRAVELED

A Jungian Psychological Perspective

*Journal Notes, Poems,
Dreams, and Blessings*

Jerry R. Wright
Jungian Analyst

 CHIRON PUBLICATIONS • ASHEVILLE, NORTH CAROLINA

www.ChironPublications.com

Cover photo courtesy of Susan Smartt
Author photo courtesy of Barbara Kovaz
Interior and cover design by Danijela Mijailovic
Printed primarily in the United States of America.

ISBN 978-1-63051-937-7 paperback
ISBN 978-1-63051-938-4 hardcover
ISBN 978-1-63051-939-1 electronic
ISBN 978-1-63051-940-7 limited edition paperback

Library of Congress Cataloging-in-Publication Data Pending

**Dedicated
In Loving Memory
To**

Kay Wright

(December 19, 1942 – April 5, 2020)

The way is ineffable.
One cannot, one *must* not,
betray it.
One needs faith, courage,
and no end of
honesty and patience.

Nature, psyche, and life
appear to me
like divinity unfolded -
what more could I ask for?

(C. G. Jung)

ACKNOWLEDGEMENTS

Among my traveling companions on this labyrinthine, mystical path called life, I want to acknowledge with deep gratitude those who have shared pilgrimages over the years, those who have attended retreats and conferences, and those parishioners and analysands who have allowed me entry into their lives and souls. You remain my primary spiritual community, although scattered throughout the nation and world. I often feel your presence along the solitary stretches of the path and my heart is warmed.

During these pandemic months of social distancing, I have been especially thankful for a few hiking companions – Barbara Kovaz, Harriett Richie, Tom Richie, and Yeardley Williams. Our conversations along Nature's mystical paths enlarged and enriched these pages. You listened patiently to my latest writing enthusiasms and offered your own reflections from your rich souls.

Thank you to friends Harriett Richie and Susan Smartt for your keen and kind editorial eyes as you read and reread this manuscript. Your patience and humor made a tedious task most enjoyable. Likewise, my appreciation extends to the professionals at Chiron Publications for making the publication maze so easy to navigate.

Finally, I am grateful for the support of friends, neighbors, and my extended family following the death of Kay, beloved wife and companion of 56 years, on April 5, 2020.

A MYSTICAL PATH LESS TRAVELED
A Jungian Psychological Perspective

INTRODUCTION

For some, perhaps the majority of persons alive today, the old religious roads in Western culture are still considered navigable and apparently meaningful.

I am not one of them.

For the first third of my life, I traveled the monotheistic Christian road that was gifted to me by family and the dominant religion of Western culture. That road provided me with a sense of community and a sense of belonging to a larger family. I learned to appreciate music and ancient stories about religious ancestors and their experiences of the holy.

Traveling that road instilled in me a curiosity for the divine—for God—who was imaged as an external, supernatural, metaphysical, interventionist Being. He was a loving Father who had one son, Jesus, who lived, died, was raised from the dead, and returned to heaven to await his return to Earth at some future date. Believing that Jesus' blood was shed for me and my sins secured me a place in heaven after my own death. You know the story ...

It is my experience that the god-image of our ancestors, and the so-called "faith of our fathers," is usually sufficient to get one up the front steps of a religious/spiritual house, and maybe onto the front porch, and even into the sanctuary. By midlife, however, many discover that their spiritual dwelling place has become too small to house the passion of body and soul, and both cry out for a more spacious container. If those cries are ignored, both body and soul will symptomize. The house will feel haunted. It is a well-known psychological law that when soul (psyche) is ignored, she will haunt us. A midlife crisis is most often such a haunting. (See James Hollis, *Hauntings: Dispelling the Ghosts Who Run Our Lives.*)

1

Widening the lens, I think our global house has become haunted since we no longer have a living myth sufficient for the modern mind and the ancient soul of our species. Collectively, we are wandering around lost and afraid—running faster, consuming more, and frantically searching for outer solutions to inner issues. Once the spirits leave a place—be it church, temple, mosque, or nation—they do not return. What remains is a ghostly haunting.

Theistic god-images, once necessary for a certain level of human consciousness, are no longer sufficient. They have effectively died, though their death remains largely ignored. We are dragging around theological and ecclesiastical corpses. Over the centuries we have tried revivals, reformations, and, more recently, louder music and larger TV screens in our places of worship, hoping to bring the deceased back to life. Resuscitation does not work. Resurrection is called for, but that necessitates acceptance of actual death, rather than thoughts or dogma about hypothetical or theoretical death.

My previous book, *Reimagining God and Religion: Essays for the Psychologically Minded* (Chiron Publications, 2018), identified the dynamics of psychological projection whereby the outer, visible world serves as a necessary reflective mirror for unconscious contents of individuals and collectives. Those projected contents, at the initiative of the deep unconscious, are invitations to recognize and integrate heretofore unconscious human capacities and potentials. Sadly, our deities and devils remain in projected forms—out there, up there, or in those we admire or despise.

Before the discoveries of depth psychology, particularly the Analytical Psychology of C. G. Jung over the last century, deities and devils were initially thought to reside in a special location in the outer environment. Later, they were moved to a metaphysical domain variously imaged as heaven or hell. Jung's genius was "the recalling of the deities and devils to their psychogenetic origins and the responsibility of dealing with them there" (Dourley 2010: 48). However, that perspective has escaped the attention of most of the world. This is especially true for theistic and monotheistic religions,

2

including the three major monotheisms—Judaism, Christianity, and Islam.

The illusion of external, supernatural, interventionist beings variously named by our species as gods and goddesses, and more recently *God,* has resulted in a pathological condition rightly described as *Monotheistic Madness.* This religious disease remains rooted in pathological tribalism—the delusion that one's tribe is the one-and-only religious tribe chosen for special favor by a one-and-only God who also provides unalterable sacred texts. Monotheistic Madness has metastasized into cultural, political, and national madness. It is of epidemic proportions. We are killing ourselves, and our environment, with these religious delusions. If left unattended, they will be fatal to our species and devastating to the Earth as we know it (Wright 2018: 39ff).

Our future depends on embracing our god-like capacities for creativity and compassion and our devil-like capacities for division and destruction. External, supernatural, interventionist saviors are no longer available, nor were they ever. Both saviors and destroyers are close at hand, in our hearts and hands. As a species we must learn to accept these parts of our own nature and live them responsibly. We can no longer outsource these innate capacities to external deities and devils. We must bring them home where they belong. Our task is to own them as members of our psychological family, individually and collectively.

As finite beings in an infinite cosmos, perhaps the greatest puzzle of all is the mystery of the human psyche, the mystery we are to ourselves. This puzzle demands our primary attention since it governs all that we think, feel, know, and choose. The health of our world, including our religions, depends on the health of the human psyche or soul.

The final pages of *Reimagining God and Religion* contained the following imaginative glimpse of our psychological and religious future:

3

Looking back from a place far down the evolutionary road, we may see the religions of the past as necessary stages along a twisting labyrinthine path toward the realization that *we are, in fact, what we imaged our former deities and devils to be.* ... Our species will come to recognize and to own both our glory and our gory that were projected, necessarily so, onto external deities and devils. In the wisdom of psyche, we will conclude that it was necessary to see our creative and destructive capacities in projected form until we could own and manifest both responsibly. Squinting, that is as far as I can see (Wright 2018: 193).

When I have verbalized this conclusion to audiences who have invited me to speak, I am met with a combination of bewilderment, disbelief, and sheer terror on the one hand; and, on the other hand, if the audience is familiar with Analytical Psychology, a knowing nod that someone has said what they have always suspected—*we have created all our deities and devils from numinous experiences that come upon us uninvited and unbidden.*

Since falling off the back porch of the Church, I am often asked, "Well, do you still believe in God?" I love the question. It's like throwing me into the proverbial briar patch with Br'er Rabbit. It is one of the most important questions at this crisis stage of the soul of our species. Rather than asking the inquirer what he/she means by the word *God* (and thereby dodging the question), I often ask a clarifying question: *Do you mean the God of the Judeo-Christian tradition? The God of the Old and New Testaments? The God of Abraham, Isaac, and Jacob?*

After receiving an affirmative response, I reply, *No, of course not!*

I then amplify: That god-image of my ancestors is no longer meaningful for me, though in my childhood and early adulthood it was the center of my religious and church life. But its shelf life has expired. It had a Best By Age 30 expiration date. After that, it was no longer nourishing; it was tasteless and likely toxic for me personally.

With the Sufi mystics, it is sufficient for me to say, *there is no god except the experience of god.* Or I echo Carl Jung near the end of his life when asked if he believed in God. His mystical reply was, "I know. I don't need to believe. I know" (Jung 1977: 428).

At this stage of my life, when I speak of *god,* I mean the animating powers and felt presences at the heart of matter itself, and at the heart of all that does matter. God is no longer an external, supernatural, metaphysical, interventionist being. That was a good story once upon a time, but these times demand more, beginning with taking more responsibility for our own god-like capacities for great good and great evil.

God is being itself—*life itself*—in all its mystical mixture, and we are its human conduit. With such a perspective, life is a mystical path—every step, every day, every moment, everywhere, and everywhen.

(Note to the reader: The following paragraph is a good example of unconscious reverie.)

Personally, the process of writing and speaking about unanswerable, yet unavoidable, questions and mysteries continues to serve the following purpose: to further free my mind, heart, and soul from the religious constraints that were a part of my religious indoctrination, constraints that remain in place for the majority of Western culture, and likely beyond, although I am no authority on anyone beyond the borders of my own skin, and even within those fleshy borders, I remain a mystery to myself, all the while proposing that I am able to see others most clearly, especially those who disturb and disgust me, their numbers multiplying daily in the weeks approaching and following a national election, an election whose outcome was foreordained to breed more chaos and contempt, a diet on which we continue to feed daily ...

I have decided to leave unedited the preceding long run-on sentence. It is in memory and honor of a most honest critic of my previous book. Still intellectually sharp at age 95, he found the book topic very interesting. When his daughter, who had suggested he read the book, asked what he thought about it, he replied, "He writes long sentences!"

I loved his assessment, first because it was true, and, second, it validates my present impulse to offer a different writing style and format. Rather than crafting long chapters or essays, I have chosen to offer brief entries from my personal journals that circumambulate the book title and theme, *A Mystical Path Less Traveled: A Jungian Psychological Perspective.* My journal has been a close daily companion for the second half of my life; we share a long, intimate relationship. My journals receive the raw materials from the unconscious, day and night, and serve as a recorder and a confessor, and preserve the inner experiences of outer events.

These brief journal entries are more conducive for what I call *magnetic reading*—allowing the words on the page to draw up within the reader his/her own words, images, reflections, and reverie. Just as my own writing and teaching constitute my own religious and psychological *testament,* the responses of the reader or audience become a part of their own testament. Our personal testament is our most valuable, and most authoritative, resource for traveling the mystical path that is our *one wild and precious life* (Oliver 1992: 94).

The writing style for this book was chosen from my own reading preferences at this stage of my life. Except for novels, I seldom read new books cover to cover. Rather, with my journal at my side, I read a new book until something within me stirs awake as if desiring expression. I then lay the new book aside, open my journal, and record what bubbles forth. This is what I mean by *magnetic reading*, sometimes called *deep reading*.

The journal entries herein have been selected from the most recent five-year stretch of my pilgrimage, beginning with the following entry on the morning of December 10, 2015:

> *Seems like each Advent my own unconscious is stirred, activated. Psychologically speaking I hear a voice: "Of course, you have been teaching, preaching, speaking about the Advent dynamic for 40 years! Except now you have a new language. The Advent is not coming down from heaven, but up from the unconscious depths." I seem flooded with passion, ideas, insights, and*

*associations which both energize me and paralyze my
writing.*

In the following five years, the flood has continued, along with my passion to record what washes up on the dry land of my writing desk. Breaking through the writing paralysis, I published some of those contents in the previously mentioned book. The present volume can be seen as a companion to that one. It contains selected journal entries over that span of time. I have edited the entries for grammar and sentence structure, although their contents remain essentially as initially recorded.

However, the brief entries consisting of a few sentences or paragraphs can be deceiving. Behind most of them are pages of labyrinthine wandering and wondering. An image or idea emerges, and I hold it up and look at it from different angles. I delight in the idea or image; I fuss at it; I ask for more clarity, and sometimes clarity is granted and at other times not. I may circumambulate the image for many pages, even over a period of days, before being able to summarize the kernel or essence. What eventually arrives on these printed pages has traveled miles before it can rest. I mention this as a confession of my own style, and as possible encouragement to you, the readers, to claim your own writing or journaling style.

Reviewing the 20 completed journals marking this most recent stage of my spiritual pilgrimage, the image of *A Mystical Path Less Traveled* emerged as a meaningful pattern of my psycho-spiritual trek. The following journal entries circumambulate that image and are in no way sequential. Again, they were, and are, more labyrinthine, winding back and forth, much like the contents of dreams. This also accounts for some repetition of ideas and themes in the following pages.

Finally, many of the major themes herein are offered in the language and style of poetry. I think of poetry as *round words* capable of holding multiple meanings. Poems are also *verbal bridges* connecting apparent opposites, giving birth to paradox, irony, and holy contradictions. Poetry may be our best language to express the inexpressible and to name the unnamable. Like music, poems invite recurring listening, and their phrases may take up residence and resonance in our soul.

In keeping with the image of a mystical path, many of the poems are indicated as *Trail Markers*. They are meant to provide maps along the way, to denote major intersections of spirituality and depth psychology, and to point along paths for further exploration.

Chapter One, titled "God and Religion Reimagined," continues some vital themes from my previous book and serves as a bridge to **Chapter Two**, "A Mystical Path Less Traveled." **Chapter Three**, "Jungian Psychology: A Modern Mystical Path," makes the case for a *psychological mysticism* that precedes and replaces a theological mysticism dependent on theistic god-images. Jung's Analytical Psychology was never intended to be a new religion. However, many find it a meaningful companion in this liminal time between old religious forms that have lost their relevance and new forms that are hopefully on the horizon.

In **Chapter Four**, I have included selected dreams from my journals that contain common or universal images, symbols, motifs, and patterns of human thought, behavior, and predicaments, i.e., archetypal. They are offered without personal context, associations, or comment. This allows the dream images and symbols to draw up within the reader that which is seeking light from his/her own depths.

Chapter Five includes an imaginative email from *Wisdom Within the Universe*. It employs a modern technological medium to update ancient perspectives about *god, religion,* and what it may mean to *travel a mystical path.*

The "Blessings" in **Chapter Six** were composed on pilgrimages to the sacred isle of Iona, Scotland, and shared at breakfast to provide a poetic framing for the day. Since one purpose of pilgrimage to places deemed sacred is to heighten our appreciation of the sacred wherever we live, the "Blessings" are now offered as morning meditations for our daily mystical walk.

The image of *roads or paths less traveled* has been employed by others, of course, most notably by the poet Robert Frost and by psychologist M. Scott Peck. Robert Frost watched as *Two roads diverged into a wood, and I / I took the road less traveled by / And that has made all the difference.* In 1978, Scott Peck's book, *The Road Less Traveled: A New Psychology of Love, Traditional Values, and Spiritual Growth,* gave early voice to a generation of spiritual seekers who could no longer find the desired spiritual nourishment in traditional religious forms and institutions. Now, 40 years later, the multitudes of spiritual seekers continue to flourish while traditional religions, and their institutions, continue to languish. Many spiritual paths have opened up for those who hunger with a longing heart and whose courage matches their hunger. The Analytical Psychology of C. G. Jung is one such path. References to Jung's *Collected Works* will include page numbers rather than paragraphs.

It has been suggested that all writing is autobiographical, and so it is, just as all reading carries the same subjective designation. In the final analysis, all writing, reading, and proclaiming about the mysteries we have designated religious, spiritual, or divine are subjective, although we seem desperate as a species to claim otherwise. This desperation has caused way too much pain, division, and bloodshed and may well be our undoing as a species.

My writing is directed to those who have a hunger for the holy, yet who no longer look to traditional religions for soul food. I am also writing for a large group of religious veterans, those who have served their time in the monotheistic tribal wars. Some, like me, served on the front lines as religious professionals. Many were wounded in those wars, with deep scars as proof; many were captured and tortured by a lifetime of unnecessary shame and guilt; some have managed to escape and now search for a spiritual worldview and a path that make tribal religious warfare unnecessary.

Drawing on the Analytical Psychology of Carl Gustav Jung, and his many interpreters and amplifiers, as well as various mystical traditions, these pages will propose an alternative path, *A Mystical Path Less Traveled.* Again, you are invited to read with your own journal in hand. The contents therein will be your most valuable, and most authoritative, resource for your own path.

TRAIL MARKER

The Road Less Traveled (Reprise)

Two roads diverged into a wood
And Frost took the difference-making one
Followed by psychologist Peck
Both explorers of poetic soul
Leaving trail markers
For future explorers.

That idyllic wood is disappearing fast
To clear-cutting and asphalt
For roads that go
Nowhere faster
And oversized houses for
Oversized egos.

Those once diverging wooded paths
Are now buried
Beneath tons of steel and concrete
In spider webs of ugly twisted art
At converging highways
Replacing the ways of bees and birds
And spiders.

Why must we faithfully execute the command
To multiply, subdue, and dominate
Yet ignore wisdom from the same book
To consider the birds of the air
And the lilies of the field
Who are Nature's
Models of trust?

Our road choices do matter
Do make all the difference
For our Mother
And her offspring
Life and death at stake
In Carson's Silent Spring.

Future generations
May well profit from the poet's wisdom
While wondering about the wooded paths
He bespoke
Lost to our lust for progress
And profit.

The way we treat the body of the Earth
Mirrors the way we treat our own flesh
And that of others
And the body politic
As outer so inner and reverse.

Consume more and more
Drill baby drill
Echoes of unconscious treatment
Of Earth
And women
And the feminine in all of us.

What trail markers are we leaving
For future generations
Should there be some
To consider diverging paths?

CHAPTER ONE

GOD AND RELIGION REIMAGINED

TRAIL MARKER

god

There is no god
except the experience of god
so says Sufi wisdom
Wisdom sorely needed in a time
when the old deities in the top rung
of a three-tiered universe
have either died or retired
Leaving heaven-hungry humans
clinging to dogmatic life rafts
barely afloat in a turbulent institutional sea.

What sounds like bad news portends
good news for those who no longer reside
in that collapsed universe
and for those who can no longer abide
a supernatural being
who has a favorite tribe
and only one son guarding the salvation gate
Creating an illusory shortage of divine water

requiring fences and secret creedal codes
Generating competition, division, and terror
and more and more weapons to protect one's god
and stories deemed sacred.

As long as our deities are supernatural beings
occupying an external metaphysical home
and intervening for our religious tribe
We will continue to do great harm
to others, ourselves, and our Earth home
While doing a victory dance
in sanctuary, field, or political hall
proclaiming we are number one
while losers weep
and plan the next inevitable battle.

We continue to spill blood
over the stories we tell ourselves
about the gods we have created
and are obliged to defend
Excusing our cycles of violence and terror
while praying god's will be done
Or God Bless America, or Allah Akbar
before lying down for fitful sleep
We will to our children our unwillingness
to face our human fears disguised as faith
Their inheritance our unlived life.

Who will have the uncommon courage
to speak common sense to our common delusions
of external magical gods and magical books
How long will we export the responsibility
for our difficult human choices to a remote deity
or to a human pope, or to a dusty paper pope
created by the Bronze-age male psyche?

Was the reduction of the many
to one supernatural male
revelation from heaven's heights
Or eruption from the human depths
of two-million-year-old fears of
shortages of god-goodies?

When will we accept that
all our gods and goddesses are
necessary symbols or metaphors
The supernatural, theistic, all-male God of Abraham
being no exception
How else can we explain so many gods
over so many years for so many peoples?

Meanwhile we humans remain innately conflicted
needing god-images to relate to the mysteries
in which we find ourselves
Yet preferring to possess the power
behind and beneath the image
When management of the mysteries
overrides trust of those mysteries
dogmatic religions are birthed
along with overt and covert terror.

Symbols and metaphors
provide a peek behind the veil
Protection from the blinding light
of the ineffable and unnamable
though we are condemned to keep trying
They remain the best medicine
for ego-inflated and power-hungry
individuals and religious tribes and nations
claiming to be founded by a god
with stamped coinage providing proof.

When symbolic gods are abandoned
to the trash heap of literalism
They become poisonous darts to the heart
and religious Kool-Aid dispensed by
self-appointed messiahs
Let us beware of any god that can be
possessed or owned or marketed
regardless of how many TV screens
are in the Sunday marketplace.

When the experiences of god are elevated
as the mystical norm
The remote gods
will be free to incarnate
Not once as rumored
but everywhere and everywhen
Every bush and person ablaze
with dazzling unquenchable light
The light of the world
no longer hidden under a bushel
as the mystical teacher proposed.

The god-experiences keep a-coming
moment by numinous moment
for those who have keen eyes
and discerning ears
They emerge not from theological heights
but from collective psychological depths
Where god-like powers and presences
actively plan their next excursion
through the thin curtain
Desiring even demanding their rightful place
in the human heart
and economy.
Why have we kept our gods

so remote for so long
And made our religions so difficult
and for so few
Would it not be more human
and humane and divine
to live *as if* we are the gods
we have created
And the devils we have shunned
Or is that asking too much
of our religious pathology
and our adolescence as a species?

This author is often accused
of using angry words
when addressing the holy business of religion
Guilty as charged your honor
having been complicit in promoting
external supernatural literal gods
Showing favor to some and shunning others
and presiding over religious corporations
too big to fail.

May these words and symbols and metaphors
be partial penance for my necessary
and unnecessary sins.

Journal: (December 20, 2015). This morning as I was showering, a question presented itself to my consciousness: *So where are you now in your relationship to the Church, your Christian heritage, and to religion itself?*

I waited for an image to appear, rather than trying to create one, and it did, although I resisted it at first. It was a *waking vision* that played out for the remainder of the shower and many minutes beyond.

No longer on the back porch of the Church, I see myself out in the adjacent cemetery where I am witnessing a massive memorial and burial service. As I allow the image to unfold, it becomes clear that what I am witnessing is a memorial and burial service, not only for the Church and the 2,000-year-old Christian myth, but the myths of other monotheistic traditions as well, each of which has been supported by a supernatural theistic god-image. Such an image is no longer viable, or even possible, from a depth psychological perspective.

As the image continues to play out before me, I realize that this funeral/memorial service has been going on for a long time. I am not the first to witness it, nor will I be the last. It appears that what is taking place in the religious cemetery will take a long time, perhaps generations. Yet, it appears that for religions to be vital and meaningful for the future, a continuous stream of religious adherents will need to make their journey to the cemetery to pay their respects for what has died; to celebrate the life that was; to mourn its demise; to endure the identifiable stages of grief, including shock and denial, anger, depression, bargaining, and acceptance; and to await a new beginning. (*End of waking vision.*)

This vision gave birth to many of the themes included in my previous book. The following is a summary of that work, along with its urgent challenge:

> With the necessary demise and death of antique cosmol-
> ogies and traditional religious paradigms dependent on
> external supernatural deities and devils, the modern
> religious challenge involves two simultaneous sacred
> endeavors: to eulogize, bury, and grieve the theistic and
> monotheistic god-images and the religious paradigms

dependent on them; and, secondly, to bring fresh imagination to the meanings of *god* and *religion* that will satisfy both the modern mind and ancient soul.

As long as our deities and devils are perceived to be beyond physical life and the life of the human psyche, our species will continue to do great harm to ourselves, to each other, and to our nest (Wright 2018: 59,39).

Journal: Before the gift of self-reflection (in the most recent 200,000 years of the 13.8 billion-year cosmic unfolding), there were no powers and presences named gods, goddesses, deities, and devils, nor theology or religion. We created those categories from our experiences of the mysteries in which we found ourselves. We did not create the experiences themselves, yet all the names and categories were from the human imagination.

The universe(s) is a metaphorical *Cosmic Canvas* whose origins are unknown and ultimately unknowable. Our species is invited, and compelled, to fill the canvas with words, images, and symbols that emerge from our unconscious depths. This ancient art is our attempt to find meaning concerning our place against the mysterious backdrop. Some of the pictures we paint are termed religious, others are considered science or art, and some are simply wordless wonder and awe.

As human creations, our pictures are temporary rather than timeless, partial rather than complete, and ever in need of updating lest they become idolatrous or objects of worship. Regular imaginative updates may be the most important task for the continuance of our species.

Again, it was we who named our felt experiences of the natural world, employing words like *gods, goddesses, spirits, demons, mana, Brahman, Zeus* and, more recently, *God*. In this sense, we created our deities and devils, and assigned names and dwelling places in the outer landscape and later placed them in heaven and hell. While creating our deities, devils, and subsequent religions was necessary, we must also confess they are "necessary fictions" that must be continually reimagined, revised, and rewritten. Religions, and the gods at their core, are human creations. This is bitter medicine for religious tribalism.

Journal: The _Cosmic Canvas_ refers to the cosmic order, the backdrop that we can only dimly divine. It is truly the Great Mystery that will remain so even as we continue to peel back the outer layers. Jung sometimes referred to this backdrop as the _psychoid level_ beneath the level he described as _archetypal_. This was his way of imagining that the collective unconscious, archetypes, and complexes rest on a larger unknown and unknowable foundation.

We keep confusing our deities and their names with the unknown backdrop. Then, in our need to protect those names, we continue to create divisive religious tribes, all the while claiming that we are defending our Faith.

Journal: The urgent dangers we humans have created for ourselves necessitate a reimagining of god and religion, whereby we are no longer children of a heavenly parent. Nor do we need an external savior who will magically rescue us. Rather, we must imagine that we are, in fact, the god-like and devil-like beings that we have long seen in projected form(s), most notably on the faces of those we idealize and/or demonize. Then, having recognized the disowned aspects of our individual and collective selves, we can take responsibility for our creative and destructive capacities. Until we do that difficult psychological work, our world will provide an unlimited quantity of scapegoats.

It seems that what has proven to be eternal for our species has been the cycle of violence caused by the gods we have created and have felt obliged to defend. Human fear and greed are older than the gods we have imagined.

Journal: Our god-images and religions seem frozen in ancient time while all else has moved on. Religion seems to be the only discipline that refuses to update itself. However, consciously and unconsciously, our god-images and religions have more powerful sway on our behavior and on our future than any other discipline. Why do we assume that our ancestors' views on the mysteries of the universe are more sacred and more authoritative than our own? We will not be able to evolve as a healthy species until our deities and devils are returned to their home in the human psyche and allowed to mature.

Journal: We create theological words, names, and doctrines and assume we know that which has been named. Yet what we know is only the name we have attached to the mystery that has come calling. That name is part of the foreground, while the background remains obscure, unknown, and ultimately unknowable.

What we do know all too well, however, are our human capacities for great good and great evil. We know this from our motivations and behavior; they are experiential facts, verified by our human history and our personal history up to the present moment. Theologically, we may speculate as to the origins of those capacities in the far-off background, yet their operations in and through the human psyche need our greater attention.

Journal: Religions have spent far too much time, energy, and ink trying to understand a supposed remote, metaphysical, supernatural, interventionist Being, and precious few resources seeking to

21

understand the human psyche and imagination that created the categories of deities, devils, and religions in the first place.

Supernatural theism seduced us away from our own nature by our trying to understand the nature of external, metaphysical, interventionist gods. In the last 100 years, Jung's Analytical Psychology can be seen as a necessary compensation for that seduction. We now know that the images of deities and devils serve as mirrors of our unknown selves that desire to be brought to consciousness; or, to employ traditional religious language, images that desire to be incarnated. Depth psychology provides a pathway to come home to ourselves, to our home in the natural world rather than a supposed supernatural one.

Journal: All last night I wrestled, Jacob-like, with the notion of external deities and devils as the cause of our shallow religion, particularly Western Christianity. The root values of honesty, kindness, civility, justice, and democracy are being traded away for the promise of greatness and given sanction by conservative Christians. We are witnessing the dismantling of human and humane values under the leadership of a cult figure. This dismantling is then given validation with "God Bless America" and "In God We Trust." Really? We have killed God with our shallow god-talk.

Our culture may be too far gone to nurture soul, wed as it is to capitalism, consumerism, and materialism. And while our culture wastes away, too many theologians continue to argue over biblical interpretations, ancient doctrines, and creeds. All of this leaves our religious institutions, in the words of the poet Rilke, like places "where God is imprisoned and lamented like a trapped and wounded animal" (Barrows and Macy 1996: 121).

Journal: We <u>are</u> the deities and devils long seen, necessarily so, in projected images and forms. Over the slow slog of human consciousness, it was necessary to see aspects of ourselves in projected forms before we could recognize them as parts of our hidden or unconscious selves. That recognition and ownership has barely begun. We seem to prefer to keep our deities and devils at a distance—up there, out there. It seems easier and safer that way. Worshipping an external god continues to be preferred over incarnation.

Journal: We <u>are</u> the deities and devils seen in projected images and forms over the centuries; yet, we have erroneously assigned/exported these unconscious aspects/potentials of ourselves to theistic and monotheistic religions as external, supernatural, interventionist beings.

It is a sad irony that the salvific term _substitutionary atonement,_ so prized by evangelical Christianity, may actually be the core issue for the destruction of our species and environment. That is, religions that substitute outer solutions to inner issues may be seductive salves for our human predicaments, yet they cannot save us from ourselves.

Journal: The theistic view of _god_ has not made our world safer, nor has it brought us closer to the metaphorical Reign of God. The last century was arguably the most violent and deadly for our species and for our planetary home. While the world has profited by advances in modern technology, compassion for each other and our environment does not seem on the rise. As long as our deities and devils are perceived to be beyond life in a remote metaphysical domain, we will continue to do great harm to each other, to ourselves, and to our fragile nest.

We are tasked with bringing our deities and devils home to the human psyche where they originated, so that we can be responsible for the powers of creativity and destruction that are in our human hearts and hands.

Near the end of his long career exploring the human soul in great depths, Jung could still write, "We need more psychology. We need more understanding of human nature, because the only real danger that exists is man himself. He is the real danger, and we are pitifully unaware of it. We know nothing of man, far too little. His psyche should be studied, because we are the origin of all coming evil" (Jung 1959: 436).

Journal: When the divine is located within matter, within Nature, and within our human nature, we are the embodiment, the instrument, the conduit of divinity—everywhere and all of the time. We have the power to heal or to hurt, to create or destroy, to love or hate, and to connect or divide.

We are then full-time religious beings. Every decision is a religious/spiritual decision. Every person we meet presents an image of the divine, whether or not the person has that self-identification.

With that orientation, that worldview and self-view, we are empowered because we have the resources to draw on regardless of the situation. We have the power of divinity itself. We have the responsibility to co-create the future. And, yes, we have the power to destroy, as well.

Some have the notion, the fear, that if there were no theistic god, then we could act as we please, and there would be no reason to act ethically. Actually, the opposite is the case. As conduits of divinity, we would bear more responsibility to behave ethically and compassionately.

We must allow our theistic and monotheistic notions of god to die so that we can claim our birthright as conduits of divinity rather than as worshippers of an external divinity.

Journal: Perhaps the world is not only in our hands, but in our mouths. Words do create worlds. The three-tiered world created by the word God, referring to a theistic being, is no longer a world that can be inhabited by modern consciousness. God has become a lazy word employed when we don't want to do the difficult work of theological reflection. It is a throwaway word, as OMG in the modern lexicon, or as a blessing at the end of a sneeze. It will be an awkward, difficult transition to find and use words and images that preserve the mysteries at the heart of life without evoking the image of a supernatural male being. Furthermore, simply altering the gender, by changing Father God to Mother God, will not be enough, although that rather recent change has validated that our god-images are undergoing an evolution.

Journal: Yesterday I was thinking that rather than writing about the monotheistic myth and god-image having died, perhaps it would be more palatable to readers to say that it has proven to be inadequate or insufficient.

However, for me that would be a cop-out. It would represent that predictable stage of grief, the bargaining stage. No, the myth and god-image have died! We must provide them with an appropriate funeral, offer heartfelt eulogies, and bury them. Nothing short of death will permit resurrection.

Many self-identified progressive or liberal theologians and authors seem to walk close to the edge of the gravesite and then retreat. The retreat comes in the form of repeating traditional references to God as an external, separate being. I can appreciate the hesitation. A lifetime of work and writing may be called into question, as well as the dismissal from religious authorities. Yet facing that question with the courage of newly found conviction might be a deeper witness to faith/trust than pleasing salutes to audiences or religious authorities.

Journal: This morning I am thinking that as bold and radical as some considered my first book to be, it was actually not radical enough. I declared that for me the monotheistic god-image and myth have died and suggested that those who remain identified with the three major monotheistic religions are likely suffering various stages of unconscious grief. Grief is natural and necessary and has no prescribed time frame. However, grief can also be a place to hide from the challenges and responsibility of embracing a new future and a new life.

The time for mourning theistic and monotheistic gods and religions has passed. Pretending death did not happen is no longer a viable option. Childish faith is no substitute for childlike faith called trust.

Journal: As an exercise of religious faith, we have to entertain the possibility that there is nothing we can do to save the Church we have come to know, even to love. Perhaps the Church has to experience its death, the very death it proclaims is the doorway to new life, and the death it fights so hard to avoid.

For me, the Church died long ago when its foundational myth was literalized and morphed into a plan for empire building and world domination. The mystical teacher, Jesus, was nowhere to be found. That Jesus remains buried under centuries of dogmatic wrangling.

Those who remain in the Church, hoping for a miraculous cure, may at best be in a collective grief support group, with its leaders providing weekly eulogies. More generously, the Church has been under hospice care for centuries, yet its members and leaders continue to ignore the DNR (Do Not Resuscitate) notice prominently displayed.

This constitutes part of my personal experience and testament. It may or may not be true for others who are equally sincere and equally deluded. It's the honest dialogue by which we approach truth that remains just outside our reach and always beyond our grasp.

Journal: Religion and spirituality are too important to leave to theologians and religious professionals. Religion and spirituality require the contributions of psychologists, scientists, anthropologists, sociologists, artists, businessmen and women, and, yes, even politicians. Self-identified atheists are also making vital contributions. If the natural, material world is truly home to the divine, all perspectives on the mysteries must be honored.

Journal: Though a radical perspective, and worthy of the designation *heresy* by the orthodox mind, theistic and monotheistic religions have been an impediment to the experience of the divine within life itself and within the human psyche. Analytical Psychology has broken through the haze, the centuries-long insulation from the divine. The breakthrough, however, requires more responsibility from our species, not less. We can no longer export our capacities for creativity and destruction to external beings, nor to those we idealize or demonize.

Journal: Now that the monotheistic deity and devil have retired to their eternal resting places, alongside their predecessors Zeus, etc., the religious question presented to us is not: *Do you believe in the God of your ancestors?* The more relevant questions are: *Will you live responsibly the deity-like and devil-like capacities within your own self? Within your own religious tribe? Within your own political tribe? Within your own nation? Within your own community?*

Journal: Patriarchal religion, culture, and politics will never be healed or transformed as long as we are devoted to a one-and-only external male deity who has a one-and-only son who is the one-and-only savior of humankind. No matter how we try to reform the old religious paradigm or to spin it with renewed or progressive interpretations, the patriarchal roots remain.

We must accept that the patriarchal temple has collapsed. Some are still sorting through the rubble trying to find signs of life. Others have turned their heads pretending not to see. Still others are searching for new sources of nourishment for soul beyond religion and spirituality.

Others of us are searching for mystical roots, not of religions, but of life itself, keeping company with mystical poets like Rilke: _I live my life in widening circles / that reach out across the world / I may not complete this last one / but I give myself to it / I circle around God, around the primordial tower / I've been circling for thousands of years / and I still don't know / am I a falcon, a storm, or a great song_ (Barrows and Macy 1996: 48).

Journal: I had an insight yesterday about our preoccupation with guns and our nation's difficulty dealing with gun safety and gun control. As long as unconscious men exercise religious, cultural, and political power, they will protect their phallic symbols—guns, knives, missiles, spires, and towers.

Unconscious men are caught in boy and cowboy psychology, strutting around with a gun on their hip and a phallus in their head. The male penis, the one between the legs, is made for pleasure and reproduction and intimacy. The unconscious penis, the one in the head, is intent on power and control and, by god, no one had better mess with that one!

Journal: When religions are uprooted from the natural world in favor of a supernatural one, and their myths are literalized, their roots bleed to death. When the blood of Jesus is literalized as an antidote for sin and a literal cup of salvation, as is the case for many, religious meaning bleeds to death. Rootless entities, whether religious or cultural, cannot thrive, or survive.

Journal: Our uprooted religions are a direct consequence of our being uprooted from the natural world itself. Furthermore, religious myths that suggest we are separate from and superior to Nature grant further permission to live with the destructive delusions.

Michael McCarthy, the British naturalist and author of *The Moth Snowstorm,* reminds us that the natural world is our Mother, our Home, and the resting places for our psyches, our souls. In an arresting comparison that comes from evolutionary biology and evolutionary psychology, he says that while we have had some 500 generations of civilization (some12,000 years), we had 50,000 generations when we were essentially wildlife! That older legacy continues to flow in our bodies and may be more important for our psyches than the more recent generations of so-called civilization. He notes that we may have left the natural world, but the natural world has not left us (Tippett 2020: Episode 869).

The neglect and the destruction of the natural world have a direct effect both on our body and psyche, likely more so than we have thus far imagined.

Journal: When deities and devils are rightly understood as human creations, and mirrors of yet-to-be known and yet-to-be owned aspects of human capacities for creativity and destruction, we will have discovered the mystical path toward Home as a species. Such a path will require us to live more responsibly, not less so as some fear. Laws that are written on the human heart, or psyche, are far more persuasive than those written in ancestral texts deemed sacred, or the laws emanating from Church councils or political bickering.

We must recover the individual art of soul-making from the big business of religion. Religions that continue to export their deities and devils to heaven and hell have become religious corporations too narrow of mind and too big to fail.

Journal: The body is the first responder to the nearness of the numinous, the sacred, or the mystical other. The mystical experience is first of all a bodily event, followed by an emotion, and concluding with a mental acknowledgement or interpretation. Yet, monotheistic religions have tended to deny the importance of the body and, more severely, to denigrate and pathologize its natural sexual instincts and expressions. In doing so, the body has been seen as an enemy to the experiences of the holy rather than its closest friend.

The mystic honors the body as the first detector and responder to the sacred, embraces psyche as the organ of relationship with the sacred, and experiences oneself as the responsible incarnation of the sacred. A grounded, embodied mystical path replaces religious highways to heaven that seek to bypass the body and the Earth.

Journal: Whatever we attribute to creation's source, whether theological, psychological, or scientific, it has taken up residence within matter, within physical life. This source is so intertwined with matter, molecules, and human flesh as having no separate operational headquarters.

The human body is the first responder of our species to the mysteries at the heart of life. As part of the Earth itself, the body is the finest tuned mystical instrument available to us. Those religions that deny or denigrate the value of the body, including sexuality, and elevate Heaven over Earth, are a danger to body and soul. The following three Trail Markers address such dangers:

TRAIL MARKER

JESUS

Down-to-earth, embodied, mystical teacher
Nature's son, friend, and voice
Employing divinity-laden soil and seed
Flowers and birds
Spit, salt, and tears
As props for the long running human drama
Played out on Nature's stage
Inviting suspended belief.

How lonely he now must be
A one-and-only savior
Exiled by creedal-crazed apostles
To a metallic three-seated
Air traffic control tower
To contemplate an unnecessary
Second Coming
And role of final judge
He decried the first time around.

How sad he must now be
His elevation to sanitized divine status
Far from humans and humus he held dear
As if his body, and ours, not sacred enough
Nor his parents' sexual intimacy
Sufficiently holy for birthing

Requiring spiritualization
To cover ancient shame.

Was his creedal exile an eternal reward
Or a sentence to irrelevancy
His life story reduced
To a few unbelievable sentences
Parroted weekly in the tribal echo chamber
Simply marking the end of the printed order
Before departing
Worship completed.

Perhaps those apostles like us
Were addressing their own unconscious
Hopes and fears and longings
For a far-off reality
Already in their/our midst
Awaiting incarnation
Our own lived creedal do-over
Saving Jesus
From his long exile.

TRAIL MARKER

Mary

Exalted above all women
Yet hidden for eternity
Behind a prophylactic veil
Declaring human body and flesh
And sexuality
Tainted by Augustinian original sin

Birthing guilt and shame
For the ages.

One wonders if she might have preferred
Her lowly human estate
Over a spiritualized and desexualized
Dehumanized elevation
Untouchable by ordinary women and men
Except by counting prayer beads
Or viewing iconic images
Of mother and child.

Why do men then and now
Religious or otherwise
Prefer their feminine nature in projected forms
Safely out there at arms' distance
Idealized or demonized
Escaping the risky and vulnerable
Tissue of sacred body
And tender solace of soul?

When the angel next visits Mary
Imploring her willingness to birth divinity
She may well decline
Preferring to be a human mother
For a human son
Rich in body and soul
Mind and imagination
Content with an ordinary miracle.

TRAIL MARKER

Joseph

Poor father Joseph
Almost written out of the script
Not privy to Mary's angelic contract
Left pondering his earthly role
And the sufficiency of his seed
While Mary pondered her
Heavenly impregnation
Both wondering why me?

He was there at the birthing
Saving his infant son
Thanks to the appearance of a dream
Only to disappear from the family narrative
Replaced by a heavenly Father
Whose business his precocious son
Needed to be about with
The Temple priests.

Was he proud of his son's holy business
With the invisible world
Or did he desire him in the family trade
Building visible things
Or was he simply satisfied
That he helped
To build his son's character?

History remains uneven
Mother Mary granted headlines
And art and songs
And sainthood

And he little more than a footnote
To the greatest story
Ever told
About the boy *he* fathered.

Upon hearing their mythologized biographies
Touting virginity and divine intercourse
Their reproductive prime now long past
Joseph looked at Mary lovingly
While a slow sheepish
Knowing grin
Covered his wise
Wrinkled countenance.

Journal: In this postmodern world, we must treat deities as psychological creations rather than as *a priori* external, supernatural, interventionist entities. Theistic religions are essentially dualistic, dividing human and divine, heaven and Earth, and body and spirit. The three major monotheistic religions create additional pathology, including the narcissism of being the chosen of a one-and-only god, followed by tribalism of us versus them, as well as escapism in the form of scapegoating and salvation from beyond. Theistic and monotheistic god-images are childish at best and pathological at worst.

Journal: Gods that are perceived to be external, supernatural, metaphysical beings quickly become literalized, domesticized, commercialized and, finally, weaponized with dogma, politics, and armaments. Phrases like *my god* or *our god* reveal an attitude of possession. It is not possible to worship or trust a god one possesses or owns. The familiar proclamations *In God We Trust* and *God Bless*

America too often mean "Our God is number one, and so are we! Because our country was founded *on God*, and *by God*, we are the favored nation, and *by God*, we plan to keep it that way!"

<u>*Journal:*</u> Unfortunately, monotheistic pathology does not stay contained in church, temple, and mosque. Like the deadly virus it is, it spreads to cultures, politics, and individual attitudes toward others beyond one's own tribe. The most effective treatment has proven to be the expansion of human consciousness in general and religious consciousness in particular.

Adherence to religious dogma, including stating again and again that *God is love,* has not, and will not, be effective. That theological affirmation may be a childish wish, yet it is not borne out by our experience of that which we have named God, or the way we experience ourselves.

<u>*Journal:*</u> The monotheistic god-image has been too light, bright, and white, and the repressed opposites are demanding their rightful place, not only in the god-image but in culture and politics. The all-good, all-bright god-image forces one to repress all the opposite energies out of sight into the unconscious. As Jung noted, these shadow elements do not disappear. The unconscious does not have a digestive tract that eliminates unwanted parts of ourselves. When the human shadow is ignored, it gains even more energy and power and manifests in destructive attitudes and behavior.

We are witnessing a return of the repressed of the sacred dark; or in alchemical language, the nigredo. America was founded and built on the backs of people of color—red, black, brown—and legitimized by a perverted image of god and religious narcissism. The treatment of people of color was America's original sin that remains unrecognized, unowned, and unforgiven.

Yet, soul will tolerate nothing less than wholeness and will protest through a variety of personal and collective symptoms. The symptoms will not be alleviated by passing more laws or by a mere change in political leadership. We must *uncurse the darkness*, beginning with how we image god and religion that determines the way we relate to ourselves, others, and Nature herself.

Journal: As Jung noted, one's true religion consists of where and how one invests his/her primary quantum of energy, rather than one's statement of belief. This applies to collectives as well as to individuals. From this perspective, a nation's budget is a moral document and, therefore, more revealing than coinage stamped with "In God We Trust."

Journal: The current evangelical and political regression is a desperate attempt to preserve patriarchal religion and culture. Old fearful white men are afraid of losing their power and privileges, supposedly gifted to them by a white theistic father-god. Religion is powerful since it links us with the supposed power attributed to the gods. Unconscious religion is deadly.

We are tasked with imagining a different god-image, one that is radically immanent rather than sitting beyond the clouds next to his one-and-only son guarding the salvation gate. Neither will it suffice to give the old male god a pair of breasts rather than a penis. Our task is daunting since nothing of great religious, cultural, or political change will take place unless we embrace new images of god and religion. We are not required to complete the task in our lifetime, yet we are not permitted to ignore it.

Journal: Last evening I heard Jungian Analyst and professor Dr. Fanny Brewster speak on the "Racial Complex." When addressing our nation's history of slavery, she repeatedly referred to our "African Holocaust." I had never heard that phrase. It has so much more power and pathos than the word slavery. Perhaps it has been used, yet my own racial complex, including my unconscious attitude of white privilege, has prevented me from hearing it.

Journal: Theistic gods and their religions have been in a death spiral for centuries and have been kept alive with mechanical life-support measures like reforms, revivals, and new interpretations of ancient texts. They have been under hospice care provided by sincere practitioners. Sincerity alone, however, is no substitute for faith, nor is it an excuse for holding onto a poor certainty rather than risking an uncertain, but potentially healing, future. Resurrection is preceded by an actual death, not simply words or dogma about the life-death-rebirth cycle that has been a cosmic reenactment for as long as we can tell.

Given the magnitude of this task, and the heavy responsibility it places on our human shoulders, it is understandable why so many prefer the religious status quo and why science is so suspect among many traditional, conservative religious individuals and groups. This suspicion then spills over to politics, where power resides.

Journal: Many liberal or progressive theologians and authors speak/write so prophetically but then feel compelled to stuff all their creative imagination back into theistic boxes. Their prophetic offerings are therefore reduced to pablum to feed the least reflective religious multitudes. In doing so, they collude with keeping the multitudes little and religiously infantilized, and with perpetuating the very religious pathology they seek to address.

Journal: Carl Jung's most far-reaching psychological insight, I think, was *the recalling of the deities and devils to their psycho-genetic origins* (Dourley 2010: 18).

That is, all our deities, devils, and religions are created through the human psyche and imagination, albeit from numinous experiences that we do not create. Such a perspective renders theistic and monotheistic god-images and religions limited, terminal, and in need of replenishing after their shelf life has expired. The three major monotheisms—Judaism, Christianity, and Islam—have outlived their Best-By dates. Their core contents have not only become spoiled but toxic, promoting narcissistic tribalism, paranoia, and scapegoating. To extend the metaphor, simply changing the packaging or covering over the expiration dates will not be sufficient.

Our postmodern challenge involves two simultaneous sacred endeavors: to eulogize, bury, and grieve the theistic and monotheistic god-images and the religious paradigms dependent on them; and secondly, to bring fresh imagination to the meanings of god and religion that could serve the ancient soul and contemporary consciousness (Wright 2018: 59).

Journal: From their beginnings, monotheistic religions were breeding grounds for pathological tribalism. The three major pathologies that continue to the present are: narcissism (*we are God's chosen people/ tribe*); paranoia (*all other tribes are suspect, deluded, or need what we have*); and scapegoating (*the real problem lies beyond our tribe in those others*).

Monotheistic pathology does not stay contained in the walls of temple, church, or mosque. Like a deadly virus, it metastasizes into all arenas of culture and politics. Even more subtly, monotheistic pathology leaks into the unconscious of individuals, poisons the soul, and promotes a worldview of us versus them.

Journal: Given the patriarchal birthing, developing, and sustaining of the monotheistic god-image, it will not be sufficient simply to change the gender of that external, supernatural, interventionist being. Changing Father God to Mother God may be a sign that something needs to change, yet such a sex change changes very little. We must relocate our deities from their heavenly houses to the human psyche, or in more poetic language, to the human heart. As that happens, the Christological mystery called Incarnation will extend from one historical person to a human assignment for all. When that happens, the philosophical Word will indeed become flesh.

TRAIL MARKER

May They Rest in Peace

Let us grant our external
Supernatural
Interventionist
Deities and devils
Their well-earned eternal rest
To Mount Olympus or Sinai or Mecca
Or wherever our imagination has so assigned
They labored far too long
At our insistent imploring with
Hands folded in pious prayer
As if to hand over
Our responsibility
For both our glory and gore
By creating a never-ending herd of scapegoats,
Divine and human.

Let us grant our god-men and god-women rest
As well
From declaring holy with magic words
Bread and wine already so
And Presence
Already always present
And forgiveness not theirs to grant.

Yet may we never rest
From embracing
Our deity-like and devil-like capacities
Long exported
Until the terror-filled trade deficit
Of our own making
Is erased
And human and humane commerce flow freely
Making way for the peace that passes
And surpasses understanding
And small
Literal
Minds.

CHAPTER TWO

A MYSTICAL PATH LESS TRAVELED

Since the words *mystic* and *mystical* likely evoke powerful emotions, images, and associations, it is imperative that I begin by clarifying my own usage of the terms. Clarifying is not synonymous with defining, however. Each of the words above denotes some form of lived experiences that resist the tight confines of definition. Such experiences can be described; description allows the experiences to continue to breathe, to continue to live.

Unfortunately, over the centuries mystics have not been granted much breathing room. Mystics have generally been marginalized by religious authorities who feel a threat to their power to determine what is holy and who can pronounce words to make it so. Many religious mystics have been deemed heretics; others have suffered death.

Mystics in other disciplines like science and the arts are often suspect as well, at least until their genius can be recognized by later generations. Copernicus and Galileo come to mind. Mystics are often considered to be strange, unusual, or odd, at least by collective norms or values. They are often dismissed as unrealistic, ungrounded, unscientific, fuzzy-minded, and more inclined toward a spiritual otherworld than this one.

My use of the words mystic and mystical, however, seeks to reverse these historical prejudices by normalizing and universalizing those experiences deemed mystical. Mystics are not a special kind of people who have unusual spiritual experiences. Rather, all people have experiences that they do not create, can't control, or command to repeat. Many of those experiences are so normal that they do not register on the traditional mystical scale, yet on reflection, they are great mysteries. From a depth psychological perspective, to be alive and to be aware of aliveness is a great mystery that qualifies as mystical. The next breath and the next heartbeat that come unbidden, the next emotion, thought, inspiration, or dread that overtake us register on the psychological mystical scale.

Widening the mystical lens, where does love come from, or joy, or depression, and where do they go when they leave? How do we stand upright while our planet spins at 1,000 mph and rotates around the sun at a staggering 65,000 mph? Where were we before being birthed, and where do we go after our last breath?

In short, life itself is a great mystery, and to be a *conscious* part of life a greater mystery still. The whole of life is a mystical path; that is, if we *pay attention*. More poetically in the words of Elizabeth Barrett Browning: *Earth's crammed with heaven / And every common bush afire with God / But only he who sees, takes off his shoes / The rest sit around it and pluck blackberries / And daub their natural faces unaware* (Browning 1992: 65).

In his mystical classic *The Idea of the Holy*, Rudolph Otto was concerned that the word "holy" had become too one-sidedly light, bright, and sanitized. He thought that holy had come to mean completely good. He created a more encompassing word, *numinous*, which expresses a wide range of human experiences and emotions that accompany what he referred to as creature-consciousness. From the Latin words *numen* (a god) and *neure* (to nod), a numinous experience is likened to *a nod from the gods* that beckons a reciprocal nod from us human creatures.

In short, creature-consciousness refers to the human experience of being in the presence of an inexpressible mystery. A numinous experience may leave one trembling or shuddering in the presence of what Otto called the *mysterium tremendum* and what our early ancestors called *daemonic dread*. On the other hand, an experience of the numinous may leave one with a sense of awe, delight, peace, or tranquility. The experience may be sudden and momentary or may last hours, days, or even longer. Numinous experiences are felt in the body and with intense emotion. A bodily response and an intense emotion become the alerts that one is in the presence of the holy, in the presence of an inexpressible mystery. Psychologically, those twin alerts denote an experience of an archetype.

Numinous experiences, experiences of the mysteries at the heart of life, are common to all and rather continuous. A mystic is one who, with creature-consciousness, notices *the nod from the gods, who sees and takes off his/her shoes*, and who metaphorically nods in return. Otto noted that numinous experiences are the foundation of all forms of mysticism, "the consciousness of the littleness of every creature in the face of that which is above all creatures" (Otto 1923: 22).

Psychologically speaking, the evolutionary gift of conscious-ness—the capacity to stand beside ourselves and reflect simulta-neously on visible (outer) and invisible (inner) reality—marks us as a species of mystics. Our sixth sense is a mystical capacity that is com-mon to all. We differ only in the value we grant it and the energy we grant its development. The exercise of the mystical gift of conscious-ness may well determine the length and quality of our stay on Earth as a species. At present, we have earned the reputation for being Nature's most creative and most destructive species. Our Mother needs us to exercise our mystical sensibilities more than ever.

Drawing on the mystical traditions from numerous world religions, on the discoveries of modern science, and on the Analytical Psychology of Carl Gustav Jung, I am proposing a *psychological mysticism* that preceded, and now replaces, the historical *theological mysticism* that has been dependent on theistic images of god. Such images are no longer meaningful for many, or necessary. These pages explore a spiritual path that has the character of a *grounded, embodied mysticism* that replaces the *heavenly, disembodied escapism* that has dominated the religious collective for more than 4,000 years.

TRAIL MARKER

We Are Born Mystics

We are born mystics
Squeezed through the thin place
in the cosmic curtain
Suddenly a lifetime threshold-dweller
between visible and invisible
light and dark
Always on the edge
of the mystical path
Animated and enlivened.

We are born mystics
Long before we are religious
or spiritual
both optional add-ons
Longer still before theism and monotheism
dominated the landscape
and soulscape
Demanding belief over experience
and tribalism over community
With holy books and holy men
given the last word.

We are born mystics
married to mystery
divorce not possible
Wed to pondering unanswerable questions
Like an unquenchable thirst
in the bar room of life
with spirits everywhere
Housed in beautiful bodies
before bottles.

We are born mystics
emerging from the pregnant
numinous darkness
into the light of day
Assigned to be and become a light
of consciousness and compassion
our primary vocation
The rent for being alive.

We are born mystics
tethered to the unbreakable holy umbilical
No redemption needed
save in the small fear-filled
evangelical imagination
infected with Monotheistic Madness.

We are born mystics
destined to be and to become
the conscious deities and devils
long seen in projected guise
Mirroring our longing-filled
body and soul
Waiting for the kairos moment
to tip the cosmic scales
with our grain of incarnated sand
Our unwritten lived creed
our best worship.

Journal: *God* was an experience, a mystical experience, long before *he* became a *he,* and longer still before becoming a team mascot for competing tribes. We were mystics long before the birth of theistic religions and long before monotheistic religions reduced the multitude of mysterious presences and powers to one. Patriarchal and hierarchal religions have overshadowed our original mystical experiences. It is time for mystics to come out of the closets to claim our spiritual birthright.

Journal: We are born psychological mystics, naturally wired for wonder, awe, and curiosity about unmediated experiences of the sacred that come unbidden. We are also wired to tell stories about such experiences. When stories about mystical moments become stories and dogma for others to believe, and are collected and canonized, those original experiences cease to be alive. They are no longer mystical; they become tools for management of a tribe or an institution. They die.

Journal: You do not have to be a self-described religious or spiritual person to have a *numinous experience*, an encounter with the holy. Numinous experiences happen to everyone equally. Such experiences meet us around each bend in the mystical path less traveled. They form the basis of ancient wisdom: *Called or not called, invited or not, the gods will be present.*

Journal: When the divine is located within matter, within Nature, and within human nature—rather than outside or beyond—the whole of life becomes a mystical sanctuary. The visible world becomes a mystical mirror. All things and all people are embodiments of the divine, a mysterious web of subjects requiring relationship.

Such a perspective is the sole basis of ethical behavior; it informs our attitudes, our behavior, and our choices. As instruments or conduits for divinity in which we are immersed, our daily living becomes our truest worship. Each moment, each encounter, each decision reveals our true worship, rather than something reserved for a special day or special place. Such a mystical perspective promotes the humility of the created, and the glory of being a co-creator.

Journal: Every religion begins with a mystical experience(s). When the mystical experience morphs into dogmatic religion, the politics of power always follows, both within the religion and within the culture of its birth. With each subsequent transition, soul suffers.

Journal: The mysterious animating powers and presences (what we humans have named gods, goddesses, and spirits) are built into the fabric of being itself. We are part of that fabric. What we have named deities and devils are mirrors of our own being seeking manifestation or incarnation. This is the mystical secret now revealed by Analytical Psychology: We are the potential deities and devils that we have longed for, long feared, or shunned. Since there are no external deities and devils, through numinous or mystical experiences, we become aware of our deepest selves that desire to be incarnated responsibly. We can no longer export that responsibility.

It is understandable why we prefer to keep our deities and devils at a distance, somewhere out there, up there, or down there. It seems safer than to wake up every morning with them in our bed, and then have them accompany us step by step, moment by moment during the day. It seems safer to reserve one hour of the week in a place deemed holy where we can pay our respects.

Journal: Psychologically, all of our deities and devils are projections and personifications, the attribution of human qualities to the mysteries at the heart of Nature and our human nature. Projections allow us to see aspects of ourselves waiting to be withdrawn and internalized. Personifications promote connection and relationship with the mysteries for the purpose of partnership. Both projections and personifications are internal psychic processes.

Journal: God-images and religions are created by the human imagination. They are inspired by numinous experiences that we do not create, can't control, or command to appear. As human creations, god-images and religions have a limited life span, perhaps several generations at most. Once primary experiences of the holy are shared, dogmatized, and canonized, they die; their death, however, may be denied for years, even generations. It seems easier to nod to the religions of our ancestors than to respond to our own experiences of the numinous, a word that means _a nod from the gods._

Journal: The mystic knows that the darkness is as revealing, and as sacred, as the light; that paradox conveys more truth than one-sided reason; that ambiguity reveals even as it conceals the underlayer of reality; that certainty is food for the religious faint of heart, while doubt enlarges the soul; and that redemption most often emerges from a most unlikely, surprising source. We love illumination and insight, yet what precedes such is most often a pregnant darkness.

Journal: A mystical path bridges all artificial divides and dualities where converging opposites give birth to paradox:
* not spirit and matter, but spirit in matter, matter suffused with spirit.

- not heaven and Earth, but heaven in Earth, and Earth suffused with the sacred.
- not divine and human, but divinity in human, and human suffused with divinity.
- not god and man, but god and goddesses in everyone and everything.

Journal: A mystical path leads nowhere fast since it is already everywhere and everywhen. There is no other place to go when the sacred is everywhere, and when every moment, every person, and every event are manifestations of the holy. The goal is not to arrive but to walk with directed attention to the where and when of the moment. The path can never be completed yet can never be abandoned except at the peril of soul. Stated another way, we are not obligated to complete our unique psychological contribution, nor are we free to abandon it.

Journal: The older I become the more I am aware that there is a mystical fool within me, at my core. Fortunately, that fool did not get analyzed away through many hours of psychoanalysis. It even survived a very traditional, conservative seminary education. It is that mystical sense that has kept my soul alive, even as it has caused my soul much anguish. For the second half of my life, I have been a mystical fool without a religious home or tribe. My fool has been on a perpetual pilgrimage. Fortunately, I have found many temporary resting places. I think of them as mystical B&Bs that provided sufficient nurture before I move on.

Journal: It may be an act of grace that we do not live long enough for all our truth to be revealed as delusions. This is what children, grandchildren, and subsequent generations are for.

Journal: Question: When did you lose touch with your natural mystical sensibilities? Your capacity for wonder and awe and attention to the little ongoing miracles? When Jesus implored, _Let the little children come to me ..._ he might have said, _Let the little mystics come to me._ He was speaking to religious leaders who had lost touch with their mystical nature due to elaborate religious rituals and laws and blood sacrifices to appease an external God.

Our lives are a series of mystical moments, yet we have grown calluses around our senses and, more severely, around our souls. The moment-by-moment miracles go unnoticed.

Journal: We are born mystics with an innate connection to the visible and invisible aspects of the one reality. Religion is an optional add-on that can secure and support that connection or damage it. Many who give up on religious affiliation have been wounded in their primary connection to the sacred. Many others keep psychotherapists and spiritual directors busy trying to undo or heal the unnecessary damage. Following a mystical path is much more meaningful than following religious roads that require tollbooths and road police.

Journal: Heaven and hell, homes to supernatural deities and devils, have been convenient hiding places for human capacities and human responsibility for both creativity and destruction. They have been closets for unconscious contents too heavy or too frightening to carry. Our collective closets are full, spilling out in all manner of individual and collective symptoms. A massive, intentional, and persistent spring cleaning may be required before our species can flower again.

Journal: We need not be surprised, though often we are, that life is full of surprises. Even though instinctually we desire safety and predictability, most of our carefully laid plans and intentions seldom unfold as we expect or hope. Ironically, surprises may be the most predictable aspect of our human journey.

Surprises challenge our illusion of control, the illusion that we are in complete charge of this one wild life that courses through us and that meets us from without. The Greeks spoke of surprises as the action of Hermes, while Native Americans attributed them to Trickster, whose purpose was to shake things up and to disturb the status quo. Serendipity is a cousin of surprise, and Jung's writings on synchronicity are a more developed member of the family.

Given the capriciousness of fate, walking the mystical path requires holding the reins of life loosely or going with the flow. Or, we could employ the religious word "trust" if we could rescue it from the common reference to assent to a set of doctrinal formulas. Wisdom suggests that we must learn to trust the mysteries rather than to manage the mysteries. The former allows us to live open-handedly, the latter requires clenched fists and teeth.

Journal: We do not need a new religion, or a reformed or transformed version of current ones. The age of traditional religions has likely passed, and those that we still cling to will likely be relegated to the museums of our species' evolution.

What we do need is a new attitude toward the mysterious life that we inhabit and to the mystery that we are. Some have called this a new religious attitude. I prefer the term mystical attitude, which moves our imagination from the deep ruts of well-traveled religious roads that have come to a dead end.

A mystical attitude allows us, and forces us, to embrace aspects of ourselves that will promote more creative and more responsible living. For example, what if we could embrace the mystical perspective that *each of us is a microcosm of what is wrong with the world,* and its corollary, *each of us is a microcosm of what is right with the world?* Such a perspective would eliminate the dualistic notions of original sin and original blessing. A psychological mystical attitude acknowledges that we are the conduits through which both creative and destructive powers manifest. Furthermore, with the hard work of consciousness, we have a measure of choice about which capacities to incarnate.

Again, what if we related to all others, both human and more than human, with the mystical attitude, *while I am not you, neither am I other than you*! (I am indebted to author and contemplative James Finley for this phrase.) Would the artificial divisions of species, genders, geographies, borders, and ideologies disappear? Would such an attitude allow us to live as an interconnected, interdependent web of being that both mystical knowledge and scientific knowledge validate?

Journal: For more than 13 billion years, there existed what we have named the natural world. When our species came online, so to speak, we gave names to our experiences of that numinous world. In this way, we created all our gods and goddesses, deities and devils, and religions. Now we are tasked with being responsible channels or conduits of those powers and presences that we discovered and named.

This is what it means to be human: to be responsible channels of the numinous powers and presences of the cosmos. In this way, we accept our role as co-creators of the future. It is a tall order, both our glory and our burden.

Journal: I have come to believe that all sin is horizontal rather than vertical. Sin is a violation of our intimate interconnection to others, to the Earth, and to our deepest self—and sometimes all three simultaneously. Only secondarily do we assign the violation to a supreme being or to a sacred teaching. Furthermore, to talk about a sin against a remote, invisible, supernatural being, and to beg for forgiveness, may well be a convenient distraction from a riskier engagement with the recipient of our offense, be it another person, the Earth, or our own soul.

Of course, this perspective locates what we have named gods within life and matter, rather than outside or beyond. It is a radical (deeply rooted) meaning of incarnation, a psycho-spiritual assignment for every person rather than one historical person considered to be the one-and-only son of a one-and-only God.

Journal: Among most religious folk, love is generally considered to be the strongest force in the cosmos, and love is what we need more of, as many songs and poems declare and most sermons conclude. After all, God is considered to be love itself. Love is a wonderful commodity, and we surely need more of it. Yet, to equate *God* and *love* does not address the age-old questions of theodicy, the why and how a loving god could permit the presence and persistence of love's opposite.

Might it be that the mystery of *life itself*, in all its mixture, remains the strongest force in the cosmos. Of course, the word life is also a human description of something unfathomable, yet it is more inclusive of that impulse at the heart of the cosmos, that impulse we have named love.

The mystic knows that the divine comes to us disguised as our life. This mystery includes all the opposites that make up what we experience as reality day by day, year by year, life by life.

There is a mystical line from William Blake that is often quoted: "We are put on earth for a little space that we may learn to bear the beams of love." Taken out of context, it is a lovely sentiment and seems to suggest a popular one-sided view of love. However, the quotation is from a poem, titled "The Little Black Boy," that captures the longing of the little boy to have his soul valued as much as the soul of the white English child. Life is more complex, more complicated than the popular view of love.

Journal: The great hesitation in abandoning the notion of god as an external, supernatural, interventionist being, seems to center on the fear that there would be no ultimate values, no order, no ethics, and the world would be a chaotic free-for-all. The expressed fear is that with no god in heaven we could do as we please without restraint. This fear reveals that god is perceived as a great rule-maker and enforcer, an image that most would deny consciously, yet may well continue to rule their unconscious.

Actually, when our deities and devils are internalized as capacities of our own psyche/soul, we are compelled to a higher ethic, rather than a lesser one. We bear more responsibility, not less. We can no longer say "the devil made me do it," nor beg god to do something that only we can do for ourselves or for our neighbor or world.

Journal: A mystical path winds its way to the *far side of complexity* where paradox, ambiguity, and metaphor reside. Over the centuries, Western religions have chosen to pitch their tents on the *near side of complexity* where literalism, black-and-white answers, and one-sided light and goodness are exalted. Those tents continue to attract millions, especially in times of uncertainty and fear.

Mystics pitch their tents on the far side of complexity, where paradox, ambiguity, and uncertainty are their daily bread. Those who find such bread unpredictable and unsatisfying reside on the near side of complexity, preferring certainty and safety, or at least the illusion thereof. Some look to religion, or religious texts, for answers to life's questions. Others look within, where deeper questions are posed for us to answer.

Journal: Why do we refer to miracles as supernatural and refer to hurricanes and earthquakes as natural disasters? One is perceived to be creative, the other perceived to be destructive. Such distinctions preserve and protect the one-sided good, light, and bright supernatural gods that we have created. When divinity is perceived to be within life, within the natural world, rather than beyond, the demon of dualism can be cast aside. Of course, as a part of that natural world, it would mean that we have to take responsibility for both our creative and destructive capacities, rather than exporting them to metaphysical beings.

Journal: For psychological mystics, the mysteries (plural) reside in matter, in the natural world, and in the moment. The mysteries are neither separate from Nature nor reserved for eternity. The time is always now, neither the distant past nor the far future, but in the _deep moment._ The deep moment contains all the past and the seeds for the future. The human psyche has access to both.

Nature consists of mystical portals through which one discovers one's self and one's true nature.

Journal: I read that the word _bereavement_ or _bereft_ comes from an old English word meaning _to deprive of, to take away, to seize, to rob._ In the midst of the COVID-19 pandemic, it is as if our lifestyles—our patterns of being and relating and consuming—all of our familiars are being taken away. They are being seized by this invisible stranger who has crossed the threshold of our homes and businesses and nations.

We are in the early stages of grief—shock and denial, anger, etc. —a grief that will likely grow more intense. We can also expect depression and bargaining. Resolution to these collective losses, of these *deaths*, may be long in coming. How do we grieve consciously to avoid more suffering that would come with denial, blame, and further distancing ourselves from each other?

Journal: We are being forced to go dormant—to wait, to be patient, to be in the darkness of not-knowing. I like that word—dormant. It's the way of Nature, yet seems so foreign to our human nature, or at least to the ways we have overridden our nature, our instinctual selves.

We are also being asked to choose dormancy, i.e., to stay at home or to self-quarantine. Dormancy carries a feeling of something necessary, and hopeful, even inviting, rather than a feeling of being robbed or punished. How might I/we embrace dormancy as a gift, an opportunity, and a necessary compensation for our otherwise incessant need to be active and busy and producing? Might there be wisdom in being forced into a condition of dormancy? How might I/we embrace this uninvited time and space as a gift?

Journal: I think of the Rainmaker story that has become a Jungian favorite. Jung first heard the story from his friend Richard Wilhelm. Jung would tell the story as often as anyone wanted to hear it. If a group gathered for dinner, Jung would say, "Did you ever hear the story of the Rainmaker?" And everyone would shout, "No! We never heard it!" And Jung would gladly repeat the story (Sabini 2002: 211).

I recently read the story again in Murray Stein's very good book *Outside Inside and All Around*:

The land was suffering from draught, so the people called for the services of Rainmaker. He came from afar, diagnosed the situation, and asked for a small hut at the edge of the city to be put at his disposal. He disappeared into it for three days, and on the fourth day the rains came. Naturally the people wondered how he was able to bring rain to their parched land. He took no credit and only said that he noticed that the country was in disorder when he came into it, so he decided to put himself in order. Naturally the rains followed (Stein 2017: 301).

During these disordering, disorienting days, what might it mean to give major attention and energies to tending our inner house, to "putting ourselves in order"? What might that mean theoretically and practically?

Journal: Perhaps Nature herself needs a rest from our incessant demands on her, our prodding her, our depleting her, our ungrateful demands that she must continue to provide more and more. She goes dormant/dark every night, and for an annual season, even as we resist the dark, both literally and metaphorically. There are large swaths of our planet that never go dark anymore. The literal lights are always on. I wonder about the effect this has on the plants, trees, animals, and migratory birds; I wonder, too, about the effect on our instinctual bodies. Sleep disorders are on the rise. We seem to be at odds with the dark at many levels. Many in our own nation remain at odds with those who have dark skin, or any skin that is not white.

Journal: It would be unwise, I think, to suggest that Nature has caused this coronavirus as a necessary lesson for our species. Cause-and-effect thinking is of little value here. However, we can speak of synchronistic events—two meaningful events coinciding that don't have an apparent causal connection, pointing "to a profound harmony between all forms of existence" (Jung 1959: 261). Such events provide opportunities for deep reflection and meaning-making.

The virus has emerged alongside a worldwide *psychic infection* whose symptoms include great collective divisions, angst, and cultural, political, and religious tribalism; and this psychic infection is occurring at a critical time for the health of our planet. Negotiating the coronavirus crisis validates the experience of what we have been saying for a long time—*we are part of an interconnected, interdependent web of being*. The virus has no geographical, political, cultural, or religious preferences. So, while Nature has not *caused* the pandemic to teach her most destructive species a lesson, so to speak, it could force us to wake up and to change our behavior. We can hope.

On the other hand, it would not be wise to attribute this crisis to the purposeful hand of a theistic God, though religious fundamentalists are certain that it is a sign of the fast-approaching end-times and Armageddon, coordinated by a supernatural, interventionist deity who, of course, favors them and their religious tribe!

The traditional monotheistic image of *God* no longer provides meaning for me, and I consider it potentially toxic to our species! I am more concerned these days with the Doomsday Clock that is currently set at 100 seconds before midnight! Our collective behavior as a species manages that timepiece, rather than a remote, interventionist deity!

I prefer a god-image that is much more intimate and inclusive of all aspects of life as we know and experience it. I prefer an image that locates the god-experience within life itself, rather than beyond or outside life. I prefer: *The experiences that our species have named gods, goddesses, and God are the animating presences and powers at the heart of all matter, and at the heart of all that does matter.*

Journal: Near the end of his life, Jung was asked about his definition of God. He replied: "To this day God is the name by which I designate all things which cross my willful path violently and recklessly, all things which upset my subjective views, plans, and intentions and change the course of my life for better or worse" (Jung 1960: 525).

Jung's definition would include all the carefully laid plans and intentions that we have had to cancel, and those that will follow. We don't yet know if what has crossed our path is for better or worse. We will wait and watch and wonder.

Journal: From these psychological perspectives, the coronavirus and its far-reaching effects could be one of the most important religious experiences of our lifetime. Of course, that perspective necessitates a reimagining of religion and god, topics that remain vital for me. To use the descriptive word coined by Rudolph Otto, and borrowed by Jung as the cornerstone of his psychological house, this crisis is a _numinous_ experience. The holy is not always bright, shiny, and uplifting, as we have been taught; it has its opposite disguises, as well. In the presence of a numinous experience, whether one eliciting awe or anxiety, we are often forced to our metaphorical knees individually and collectively. In this posture of worship, we are forced to confront our illusions that we are independent, self-contained, autonomous, rational beings in need of nothing more than more and more.

Journal: Where can we turn for help in these desperate days? To current politics? Hardly! To new elections and new leadership? Probably not. New leaders may stop some of the bleeding, but our deep divisions will continue until the underlying psychic epidemic is sufficiently addressed. Can we look to economics and consumerism? Both have been unmasked as very fragile! Can we find help in monotheistic religions and supernatural, interventionist saviors? They are no longer relevant, impotent at their best and toxic at their worst. All three—Judaism, Christianity, Islam—suffer from Monotheistic Madness, the delusions of being the one-and-only chosen tribe of a one-and-only God, along with a creation myth that promotes our species as separate from and superior to the natural world. These religious delusions are at the core of our psychic pandemic.

Nature and COVID-19 may have something to say about these religious delusions!

TRAIL MARKER

Monotheistic Madness

Necessity, they say, is the mother of invention
Religions not excluded
Meaning–making the inventive force
Along with security
For awe-wired fear-filled
Two-legged mammals
Treading a vast terrain
Under a vaster
Sky.

Deities and demons once spied
Everywhere
In Nature's glorious gardens
Imaginative helpers and hindrances
Granting Homo sapiens
And theistic religions
A reason to be.

Monotheists later went mad
With claims of being
The one-and-only chosen tribe
(Thrice in succession)
Of the One-and-Only
Including
The possessors and dispensers of
Unchangeable truths
Carved in stone and permanent ink
Promoting narcissism, paranoia, scapegoating.

Attempts to control Monotheistic Madness
By reform and revival
And new spins on ancient texts
Have failed
The divisive disease
Metastasized
Contaminating cultures and politics
And family tables.

How will we ever be one family
When only a few are chosen
When only a few are given
The keys to unlock theistic doors
Where the human imagination
Is held hostage
To psychological complexes
Idealizing out there
The lonely orphans
In here?

The theistic imagination
Requires a do-over
External deities and devils
No longer believable

Nor necessary
Shelf-life long past
Best-By date faded
Underneath health warnings
To conscious consumers
Of spoiled contents
Dangerous to body and soul.

The monotheistic foundation stone
Of chosen-ness
By a preferential deity
Must be excavated and crushed
Into glass
For psychological mirrors
For viewing
The multiple chambers
Of the human heart
Housing love and hate
Light and dark
Reflected off the faces of
Heroes and enemies
Human and divine.

Perhaps theism and monotheism
Were necessary stages
Along the dimly lit religious path
And the barely lit religious imagination
Slowly unfolding
Still squinting
To see the dawn
The promised light
That we are
The shining ones
Long awaited
Emerging from the dark unconscious.

Journal: Rather than dismissing the virus as an enemy to be fought and conquered and then celebrated as a war victory, we would be better served to ask for its possible meanings, even as we take elaborate steps to heal its deadly effects.

We are now being forced to face our limits, our finitude. We are being asked to confront our individual and collective addictions to more and more, our delusions of ever-upward progress, and our demands on the Earth that she be a never-ending provider. The grinding wheels of commerce and consumption, our hurrying to and fro, are coming to a standstill. Standstill—a good word, and good counsel when we feel lost in the woods, or when we have lost our way as a species. What might be the possible meanings of this kind of forced stillness in a culture/world committed to perpetual progress and perpetual motion?

Journal: May these dormant days allow us to go deeper into our inner world so that we can respond creatively to the outer chaos that touches all of us. As we guard ourselves from a contagious virus, may we embrace the wisdom of the Rainmaker "to attend our inner house." May we trust that individual psychic balance, along with compassion and hope, are also contagious!

Journal: Almost overnight we have before us—right in our faces—an archetypal image, a worldwide emotionally laden symbol: masks or facial coverings. To wear or not to wear, and where or when, are in our conversations and arguments, and now in our laws that are welcomed by some and resisted by others. Something so simple has quickly become so divisive; something so flimsy has quickly become politicized and weaponized. These reactions alone alert us to the probability that the real issues are behind and beneath our masks.

This worldwide nightmare, and its powerful symbol, scream at us, "Pay attention!" Psyche/soul meets us from without (in history, culture, politics, etc.) as well as from within. More accurately, since soul has no geography, she approaches from the visible world as well as from the invisible world. Better yet, there is only one world, one reality, considered from different vantage points. Soul work includes everything we do, desire, and hope for, whether visible or invisible.

Journal: Jungians know the value and power of symbols, and the role of our psychological masks, our *personas*. Personas—the faces we turn toward the visible world—are natural and necessary. They <u>reveal</u> something of who we are, especially when we need to play appropriate roles for social engagement. Personas are necessary for efficiency, productivity, and even politeness.

Our personas also <u>conceal</u> aspects of our personality; they protect us from being too vulnerable, too exposed, especially in hostile environments. However, our masks also <u>conceal</u> the more unsavory aspects of our individual and collective shadow. They can serve as hiding places not only from others but, more severely, from ourselves. *It is what we hide from ourselves that is most damaging to our soul, and the soul of the Earth and world!*

Journal: What if we consider the pandemic for the dream/nightmare that it is, along with its core image, masks? Since dreams generally reveal something not yet known or are compensatory to a conscious situation to bring psychic balance, what is it that we don't know, or don't know sufficiently, or don't want to know? Or that we are afraid to know? Where are we out of balance, individually and collectively, that this worldwide crisis (this daytime nightmare) may be addressing?

What might this pandemic, and our obsessions and conflicts over masks, have to teach us about ourselves, about our relationships with each other, and our relationship with the natural world?

The depth psychological question might be: *What is seeking to be* unmasked *at the initiative of the deep unconscious that we now need for our next stage of consciousness, individually and collectively? What is being* unmasked, *or revealed, that we have hidden from ourselves, that symptomizes in our many deep divisions as a species?*

Journal: Our collective masks are being ripped off to expose our long-standing, dehumanizing history around slavery and our treatment of indigenous peoples, even as we claim "American exceptionalism" and our being a light to other nations. We are being forced to face deeper levels of our many divisions and conflicts that we have covered over, or *masked,* or hidden from our conscious view far too long: racial prejudices and inequalities, economic disparities, patriarchal and gender biases, political divisions, justice rendered to the well-to-do and the well-connected, the impending climate/environmental crisis—to mention a few. Each and all of these issues are now right in our faces, so to speak, more visible to the naked eye peering from behind our masks. Whether they are more conscious is another question. Psychological consciousness implies not only awareness but integration of awareness that alters one's worldview *and* behavior. Only time will tell. Sadly, while our collective masks of denial are being ripped off, new conflicts surface immediately over the need to don protective masks!

Journal: Before, behind, and beneath the *biological pandemic,* there lurks a *psychic pandemic* of long standing that demands our attention and continuing commitment to growth in consciousness. Jung spent his career addressing this deeper, even deadlier, pandemic, often attributing it to a loss of soul. The deeper and deadlier malady and its treatment gave rise to depth psychology in general and Jung's Analytical Psychology in particular.

Loss of soul, like COVID-19, is of pandemic proportions and knows no cultural, political, or religious boundaries. It is even more difficult to treat since its symptoms are most often masked, manifesting as anxieties and fears, cultural/political/religious tribalism, paranoia, conspiracy theories, scapegoating, and apocalyptic obsessions. These devil-like symptoms, rooted in our shadow and complexes, lurk just beneath our individual and collective personas or masks, just waiting for an opportune time to *reveal* themselves. Now is such a time.

Journal: As if describing the current daily news, Jung notes that the unacknowledged human shadow "disorders the brains of politicians and journalists who unwittingly let loose *psychic epidemics* on the world" (Jung 1957: 37). Each of us likely has particular politicians and journalists in mind who fit that bill! However, upping the ante, because of the internet and social media, we must confess that all of us are potential politicians and journalists who contribute, unwittingly, to the psychic sickness, or to its antidote. There is much to critique, even to condemn, in the blatant inhuman, unjust, and crazy-making chaos that surrounds and suffocates us. We cannot be silent, because silence conveys agreement, lack of concern, or lack of courage. However, our right to speak up and to speak out rests with our honest appraisal of our own complicity in creating the mess we are in. *What we refuse to face inside meets us from the outside as fate.*

Journal: Every day our collective behavior becomes more unbelievable, more irrational, and more dangerous. Reason, common sense, and common decency have gone into hiding.

C. G. Jung warned of the dangers of *psychic epidemics* that underlie all other catastrophes, including biological pandemics. Calling for more intensive study of the human psyche, he wrote:

> It is my conviction that the investigation of the psyche is the science of the future ... it is becoming ever more obvious that it is not famine, not earthquakes, not microbes, not cancer but man himself who is man's greatest danger to man, for the simple reason that there is no adequate protection against psychic epidemics, which are infinitely more devastating than the worst of natural disasters. The supreme danger which threatens individuals as well as whole nations is a *psychic danger*. ... The greatest danger of all comes from the masses, in whom the effects of the unconscious pile up cumulatively and the reasonableness of the conscious mind is stifled. (Jung 1958: 589).

Journal: Many, if not most of us, are experiencing symptoms of trauma—anxiety, depression, rage, bodily ailments, and hopelessness. We are exhibiting familiar symptoms of PTSD, except in this case *P* does not denote *Post*, but *Present* and *Persistent*. We are being bombarded daily by traumatic news and terrifying events that keep our bodies and psyches on high alert! We are trauma victims of the twin pandemics, biological and psychic. The damage to body and soul, immediate and long term, remains unknown.

Journal: I have been thinking of our nation as a dysfunctional family in need of "family systems therapy." The members of our national family live with the daily and hourly trauma perpetuated by an emotionally unstable, tyrannical, abusive *presidential father.*

In such an individual family, each member must devise ways to remain safe if they are to survive the horrors. Some disappear into depression, substance abuse, or acting-out behaviors, and become the identified patient often seen in family therapy. Others, often the mother, assume a rescuer role to keep the children safe, but in doing so loses her larger identity and opens herself to more abuse. Another child may disappear into books and take on the role of family scholar or later enter a helping profession, a familiar vocational choice.

The most perplexing roles to an outside observer, however, are members of the family (or the family as a whole) who become identified with the abuser as an unconscious attempt to remain safe and to preserve the dysfunctional family secrets. They end up protecting the abuser who renders so much abuse. This latter dynamic helps me understand why so many of our citizens and political leaders remain loyal to the emotionally unstable, tyrannical, abusive presidential father. Fear is a powerful motivator, often over-riding more rational functioning, as well as religious convictions.

Continuing the analogy, in such a situation, a family intervention is often necessary to address the pathology, to break through denial, and to restore health to the individual members and to the family as a unit. The recent impeachment process was such an attempt, yet it was sabotaged by more than half of the family leaders trying to save their political lives. However, for an intervention to be effective, the interventionist must be totally objective, or neutral, to facilitate the process. Neither political party, nor any of us citizens, can claim such objectivity! Certainly not I! We are equally blind to our shadows, to those things we have masked.

Maybe COVID-19 could be considered an objective interventionist, forcing us to face our individual and collective dysfunction and pathology!

Journal: It seems psychologically significant that many/most are placing hope in a vaccine to allow us a quick return to normal.

While I, too, desire a quick, effective vaccine, I am suspicious about yet another quick fix that perpetuates the familiar "external savior complex," and relieves us from having to make changes in our attitudes and behaviors. The biological pandemic invites us to see the interconnected, interdependent web of being that we are and to imagine living that way if we are to save ourselves and our nest. What we have named salvation often comes to us from the most unlikely sources.

Journal: There is no vaccine for the psychic pandemic: It does not respond to religious dogma, religious indoctrination, or religious ignorance. The only antidote is the scary, difficult work of soul, a deeply spiritual lifelong process informed by depth psychology. It involves the honest, difficult, and scary work of looking behind our own masks and taking responsibility for our bright and dark shadows—or, in traditional religious language, for our capacities for great good and great evil. I take it one step further by suggesting that *we are the deities and devils* that we have long seen in projected forms. Stated another way, each of us is a microcosm of what is right with the world, and each of us is a microcosm of what is wrong with the world. Of course, our greatest challenge is to live *as if* that were true. To do so requires great faith, understood as trust; and hope, understood as our willingness to do our part in creating a better future. In addition to faith and hope, love could be added when understood as the inclusive, active attitude that *what happens to you makes a difference to me.*

Journal: Personally, I am no longer concerned about a supposed external, supernatural, interventionist deity, including external saviors and devils. I am most concerned about the deity-like and devil-like capacities we humans possess, the lack of consciousness of this psychological fact, and the almost universal abdication of our individual responsibilities for these capacities to religions, political ideologies, and various isms.

Stated another way, we need to stop spending so much of our time and energy trying to discern the character, will, and purpose of supposed external deities and devils, and devote that same energy to understanding the human psyche. We need to stop praying to external deities for help to clean up the messes of our own making and cease preying on each other and our fragile, limited Earth.

The old, supernatural, interventionist gods that we imagined, named, and have kept at a safe distance can no longer help us. We must bring them home to the human psyche, where they originated and where they belong. They have been orphaned too long, and so have we as a species. As radical and insensitive as it may sound, we must say goodbye to "Our Father in Heaven" and assume our parental responsibilities. Sadly, we "Children of God" must grow up.

Journal: The mysterious animating presences and powers (what we humans have named gods, goddesses, and spirits) are built into the fabric of being itself. We are part of that fabric. What we have named deities and devils are mirrors of our own selves that seek manifestation or incarnation. This is the mystical secret now revealed: _We are the potential deities and devils that we have longed for, long feared, or shunned._ Since there are no external deities and devils, through numinous or mystical experiences, we become aware of aspects of our deepest selves that desire to be incarnated responsibly. We can no longer export that responsibility. The 2,000-year-old Christian myth sniffed the incarnational imperative but limited it to one historical person. That imperative, that invitation, belongs to each of us.

Journal: When the divine is located within matter, within the natural world and within the human psyche, rather than outside or beyond, the whole of life becomes a mystical sanctuary. All things and all people are embodiments of the divine, a mysterious web of subjects requiring relationship. This perspective is the sole basis of ethical behavior. It informs our attitudes, our behavior, and our choices.

As instruments or conduits for divinity in which we are immersed, our daily living becomes our truest worship. Each moment, each encounter, each decision reveals our true worship, rather than something reserved for a special day or special place. Such a mystical perspective promotes the humility of the created, and the glory of being a co-creator.

Such a mystical perspective may allow us to listen to the current pandemic with different ears, to see it through different eyes, and to remove our masks of delusion designed to keep us separate and superior to Nature, and to each other.

Journal: We come from mystery and return to mystery, and in between we breathe mystery. We may attempt to ascend or descend the great unknowns and unknowables, or to pad ourselves against their capriciousness. With our naming, we may seek to control, manage, or to placate the mystery at the center. We may try to meditate ourselves into or from it. Yet, all the while and with all our efforts, we still don't know from whence we have come and where one day we will return.

The mystical perspective leaves mystery intact while we do our best to be responsible for the privilege of whatever years, and whatever measure of choice, we may be granted. This seems to be the least we can do, and the most.

At its best, religion does not seek to solve the mystery in which we reside and of which we are a part, nor does it make the mystery more manageable. It merely provides a myth and accompanying rituals to live into the mystery responsibly, i.e., to be a conscious conduit for the powers and presences that are always seeking us out. The question posed to us on the mystical path that undergirds and fuels our true vocation or calling may be stated, *what wants to enter the world through me?* (I am indebted to James Hollis for this provocative question.)

TRAIL MARKER

Mystical Path

A mystical path
May be more desirable for those
Desiring to be more human
Rather than more religious or spiritual
The latter two being detours
On the long journey home
To our common humanity
Our most sacred inheritance.

Religion and spirituality are generally designed
To take one up and away
From the ground of being itself
Machinations to make one fit
For the great Eye in the Sky
An Eye that has gone to sleep
No longer on duty.

That God can no longer help us
No longer hears our prayerful pleas
To do for us
What we must do for ourselves.

That God is no more and never was
His ghost summoned

By those needing to feel special
While arguing over creation myths
And who is in and who is out
And who will be saved in the end
And who will be left out.

Those we have named gods
Were never in the saving business anyway
The only thing lost
Being the creative imagination
Sacrificed to me-my-mine-our
Of tribalism.

We have created problems
Only we can solve or not
Intervening gods having moved on
Leaving us children
The possibility of growing up
Or not
Of being more human
Or less than.

CHAPTER THREE

JUNGIAN PSYCHOLOGY:
A MODERN MYSTICAL PATH

Two experiences from the life and work of C. G. Jung provide the framework for these journal entries that circumambulate my claim that Jungian psychology can be considered a modern mystical path—that is, if mystical is understood in its natural and rich psychological sense.

One experience comes from Jung's childhood and the other from his mature years. Both experiences are rightly mystical in character and impact. The first is a daytime vision and the other a dream. Both experiences are very familiar to Jungian readers yet bear repeating for their potential wisdom.

At age 11, while walking home from school past the Basel Cathedral, Jung had a vision that haunted him for days. He was in torment as he tried to avoid thinking a thought/image he was convinced would send him straight to hell. Finally, in his own words:

> I gathered all my courage, as though I were about to leap forward into hell-fire, and let the thought come. I saw (again) before me the cathedral, the blue sky. God sits on his Golden throne, high above the world—and from under the throne an enormous turd falls upon

the sparkling new roof, shatters it, and breaks the walls of the cathedral asunder (Jung 1965: 39-40).

The mystical impact of this unsolicited, uninvited image given to a young boy more than a hundred years ago continues to be relevant for our modern predicament. In the earthy language of John Philip Newell:

We are living in the midst of the great turd falling! It has already smashed into the spire of Western Christianity. ... as long as we allow our spires to give the impression that God is primarily above and beyond the earth, in opposition to what is deepest within creation and in the body of the human mystery, then our spires are going to crumble (Newell 2011: xviii).

Meanwhile, many await the emergence of a new metaphorical Cathedral, one that can house fresh images and meanings that can speak to our modern minds and ancient souls.

The second mystical experience involved a dream of Max Zeller, a Jungian analyst who had spent six weeks in a Nazi concentration camp. After his release, he emigrated to London and later to Los Angeles, California, where he was instrumental in founding the C. G. Jung Institute. In 1949, he returned to Europe preoccupied with one burning question: *What am I doing as an analyst? With the overwhelming problems in the world, to see 20 or 25 patients, that's nothing. What are we doing, all of us?*

On the night before he returned to Los Angeles, Zeller had the following dream that he shared with Jung the next morning. Here is the dream:

A temple of vast dimensions was in the process of being built. As far as I could see—ahead, behind, right and left—there are incredible numbers of people building on gigantic pillars. I, too, was building on a pillar. The whole

78

process was in its very beginning, but the foundation was already there, the rest of the building was starting to go up, and I and many others were working on it (Zeller 1975: 1-5).

While discussing the dream, Jung offered, "Ja you know, that is the temple we all build on. We don't know the people because, believe me, they build in India and China and in Russia and all over the world. That is the new religion. You know how long it will take until it is built? ... About six hundred years" (Zeller 1975: 3).

Max Zeller later wrote, "There was the answer to my question what we, as analysts are doing. ... That is what happens in our work. ... We see it every day. ... Each person works on his own pillar, until one day the temple will be built" (Schweizer and Schweizer-Vullers 2017: 11-12).

Some 40 years ago, when I first read the conversation between Jung and Zeller, my initial response was disappointment bordering on despair that the work will take so long. At that time, I was a young Presbyterian pastor, fresh out of seminary, with an inflated sense of my omnipotence and omniscience. I was certain that with a little cooperation from my parishioners I/we could bring in the long-awaited "Kingdom." I gave it my best efforts and finally was defeated, rightfully so, and thankfully so.

Even now as I write this, the archetypal images and processes in Max Zeller's dream continue to speak to me personally and professionally. They remind me that the foundation for a future metaphorical temple is already in place. There are many at work in this essential, sacred endeavor. Some are known; many others remain invisible. I desire to be among them with whatever contribution I may be able to make.

Furthermore, there is a larger, greater, unfolding process that has been at work for at least 14 billion years, call it what we may. At this stage of the mystical path, I prefer the psychological metaphor *Self* rather than the theological metaphor *God*. The archetypal image Self is not limited to any particular religious or cultural tradition; it is more difficult to literalize, or domesticate, or militarize. Self is not limited by gender and does not carry all the centuries of worn-out God-talk.

In my more creative moments, I watch what is going on in my own personal world and psyche, and in the larger world that is now right before our eyes. As I watch and wait, a recurring question plays around the edges of my mind and soul: *I wonder what the Self is up to?*

Expanding the question, I ponder: *What may be emerging from the deep unconscious that is trying to get the attention of individuals, religious groups, and nations? What new images are already emerging that may give us clues to the tectonic shift that is taking place in the deep unconscious, a shift that we feel in our bones, in our souls, in our pocketbooks, and in our nation and world? And how might I/we cooperate with the new life that is trying to be birthed?*

Of course, none of us knows the precise answers to such questions. Yet none of us is exempt from asking the questions, wrestling with their unknown references, and taking responsibility to share our truth, however partial.

In recent time, as I have scanned the religious, cultural, and political horizons, the images that have caught my imagination as possible ways forward have included *psychological mysticism, a mystical path less traveled,* and *Jungian Psychology: A Modern Mystical Path.* The following pages elaborate and circumambulate these images.

Carl Jung had a complex relationship with mystics and mysticism. The complexity was not related to human experiences that he considered mystical. For him, those psychological experiences were normal, natural, and a common feature of the human condition. Mystical experiences are rather continuous if one has the awareness and a language to welcome them. His difficulty with the words had to do with those who used mystic and mystical to demean and to discount his psychological perspectives and his identity as a scientist.

Psychologists and theologians who were either threatened by Jung's work, or who failed to understand his depth psychological premises, often dismissed him with charges of being a mystic and his work as "nothing but" mysticism. Psychologists accused him of being unscientific, unrealistic, ungrounded, wooly-minded, and unduly concerned about a spiritual otherworld. Theologians often misunderstood his perspectives on the innate religious function of the psyche, claiming he had reduced God to a psychological function rather than preserving God as the Supreme Being of the Universe. Jung's dialogues with Martin Buber and Victor White clearly demonstrate the incompatibility of his understanding of the religious psyche with both Jewish and Christian monotheism (Dourley 2014: 17).

Having to defend himself from unfounded charges over a long period of time brought out sharp rebuttals. In the 1957 Richard Evans interview, Jung, now in his 80s, remarked, "Everyone who says that I am a mystic is just an idiot. He doesn't understand the first word of psychology" (Evans 1981: 147). Jung's identity as a physician, scientist, and an empiricist was paramount. Complicating the larger picture, of course, was the depth of Jung's own mystical sensibilities, albeit thoroughly grounded in Nature and human nature rather than in a remote deity.

In his 1935 lectures at London's Tavistock Clinic, lectures that remain one of his best introductions to Analytical Psychology, Jung was asked about mysticism. His reply: "Let us assume that you mean people who have mystical experiences. Mystics are people who have particularly vivid experiences of the processes of the collective unconscious. Mystical experience is experience of archetypes." He added that he made no distinctions between mystical experiences deemed to be religious or psychological (Jung 1935: 98-99). Since Jung himself had "a particularly vivid experience of the processes of the collective unconscious," he would, by his own definition, be a mystic (Lachman 2010: 2-3).

Aniela Jaffe, a longtime collaborator of Jung, begins her book *Was C. G. Jung a Mystic?* with the following: "C. G. Jung did not like to be regarded as a mystic: he preferred to be recognized as an empiricist, i.e., a scientist whose research is based on a careful observation of facts. ... Nevertheless, the clear analogies that exist between mysticism and Jungian psychology cannot be overlooked, and this fact in no way denies its scientific basis" (Jaffe 1989: 1). Jaffe acknowledges that Jung's psychology paints a picture of humanity in its essence as *homo mysticus* (Dourley 2014: 36).

Although Jung might balk at the designation of being a modern mystic because of the reasons just mentioned, mystical describes accurately his appreciation of the mysteries of the human psyche he encountered throughout his life. *The Red Book*, one of his personal journals during and after his descent into the psychological depths, has already taken its rightful place among the mystical writings of the ages.

I am proposing that Jung's extensive collective writings provide a unique witness to a *psychological mysticism* as compared to a *theological mysticism*. The powers and presences that he personally encountered, and those reported by classic mystics like Meister Eckhardt, Jacob Boehme, and Mechthild of Magdeburg, were considered to be *holy immanent* rather than *wholly transcendent*. Jung was keenly interested in their reported experiences as evidence of the symbolic processes at work in the psychic depths, rather than in their theological interpretations of their experiences.

Such a distinction supports what I am proposing to be a grounded, embodied mysticism as opposed to a heavenly, disembodied escapism. The latter continues to plague monotheistic religions and their followers, regardless of efforts to spin the outdated worldview and myth.

In this highly charged interim time between one myth that has died and the other yet to be born, I am convinced that Analytical Psychology, begun by Jung and continually evolving in depth and breadth, will be a foundational pillar for the metaphorical temple of Max Zeller's dream. Jung, the mystic, had a deep respect for the mysteries of the inner and outer world. Through his voluminous writings, he left his own trail markers for future explorers of those mysteries. Like all living entities, including religions and religious myths, Jungian psychology will also be replaced by something even more relevant and life-giving.

In the meantime, the Jungian perspective offers a reliable contemporary map for negotiating both visible and invisible domains, and for locating oneself in a meaningful way on the metaphorical threshold. (See Murray Stein, *Jung's Map of the Soul,* 1998.) The following Trail Markers and journal entries propose *Jungian Psychology as a Modern Mystical Path.*

TRAIL MARKER

Numinous

Numinous ...
A mystical nod from the gods
Coined by Otto, borrowed by Jung
Cornerstone for his personal and professional
Psychological house
Experiential balm for the
Ailing soul.

Numinous ...
Equal nods to all
Religious or non
Theists, atheists, nones alike
Color and credentials left unchecked
On the border between
Visible and invisible.

Numinous ...
Holy visits
Uninvited, unknown
Unmediated, unmistaken

Unnamable
Symbols, metaphors, and images
Sufficient.

Numinous...
Activated body and intense emotions
The first responders
Announcing invisible visitors
Bearing gifts
Sometimes desired
Always needed.

Numinous...
New word for ancient universal experiences
Baptizing low as well as high
Dark as well as light
Flesh as well as spirit
Sacred homes for the
Holy.

Numinous...
Holy retrieved from the heavens
Providing muddy shoes
To complement the halo effect
Ordinary moment by moment
Miracles
The most believable kind.

Numinous...
Ordinary mystics invited
To exit their closets
To claim standing place and voice
In the crowded religious marketplace
Selling no dogma nor doctrine
Except *I know*.

Numinous ...
When the gods come a-nodding
On the mystical path less traveled
A humble reciprocal bow
Or seventy times seven
Will suffice
To mark all places and all times as holy.

Journal: For the psychiatrist Carl Jung, the healing factor was the experience of the *numinous,* a word he borrowed from Rudolph Otto, who coined the word 100 years ago in a book titled *The Idea of the Holy.* Otto had become concerned that the word "holy" had become associated with a narrow band of life experiences that were one-sidedly light, bright, and uplifting. Numinous includes such experiences as well as their opposites.

In a letter to Mr. P. W. Martin, August 1945, Jung wrote: "You are quite right, the main interest of my work is not concerned with the treatment of neurosis but rather with the approach to the numinous. But the fact is that the approach to the numinous is the real therapy and inasmuch as you attain to the numinous experiences you are released from the curse of pathology. Even the very disease takes on a numinous character" (Jung 1973: 376-77).

Journal: I am making the case for a *psychological mysticism* rooted in unmediated, numinous experiences. Such experiences:

- are universal, common to all regardless of culture or religious identity or lack thereof;
- appear bidden or unbidden, called or not called, invited or not;
- do not require belief in an external, supernatural, interventionist deity or deities;

- do not require a supernatural savior, messiah, or mediator;
- do not require a human mediator, or an infallible sacred text;
- register first in the body, validating the body as a sacred vessel;
- are multivalent, nondual, including ecstasy and terror, delight and dread, light and dark, and what we experience as both good and evil.

Journal: Numinous moments are human universals, experienced as spontaneous presences or powers. They come unbidden. They wash upon our souls' shores, continuously lapping at us wavelike, sometimes gently and at other times with hurricane or tsunami force. They do not respect geographical boundaries, or ask for a religious ID, or adherence to dogmatic beliefs. As such, the experience of, and respect for, the numinous provides a sacred path beyond divisive, tribal religions that threaten our species and planet.

Journal: For many years I have referred to Jungian or Analytical Psychology as a religious psychology. This designation grows out of Jung's perspective that the human psyche is gifted with a religious or meaning-making instinct comparable to other natural instincts like hunger, sex, safety, etc. More importantly, it grows out of my appreciation of Analytical Psychology as a resource for meaning-making, especially in the last half of my life. Religion at its best serves this vital human task, but when any religion or religious myth loses that capacity, it ceases to be true to its name.

In more recent years, I have begun to refer to Analytical Psychology as a mystical psychology and to its theory and practice as resources for a Modern Mystical Path. Furthermore, to differentiate such a practice and path from well-worn traditional religious paths that no longer feed my soul, I employ the phrase "Jungian Psychology: A Modern Mystical Path Less Traveled." Again, each of these designations represents continuing efforts at meaning-making, of locating my one particular life and purpose to a larger whole.

Journal: From a psychological mystical perspective, life is one continuous, interconnected whole, which has evolved in five stages:

(1) Cosmic Life: Cosmic Life began at least 13.8 billion years ago.
(2) Biological Life: Biological Life began approximately 3.5 billion years ago, about 1 billion years after the birth of our galaxy and Earth.
(3) Psychological Life: Psychological Life began with the birth of human consciousness approximately 200,000 years ago.
(4) Religious Life: Formal religions like Hinduism appeared about 6,000 years ago, preceded by animism. The roots of Judaism appeared approximately 4,000 years ago; Buddhism began approximately 2,500 years ago; Christianity was birthed about 2,000 years ago; Islam began approximately 1,400 years ago.
(5) Mystical Life: The foundations are being laid for a future myth described herein as _psychological mysticism._

Journal: Psychological mysticism suggests that we meet god disguised as our life, in all its mixtures and textures. It is a practical or pragmatic mysticism that embraces _what is,_ and how we live _what is_ responsibly.

This validates Jung's response when near the end of his life, he was asked about his definition of God. His reply: "To this day God is the name by which I designate all things which cross my willful path violently and recklessly, all things which upset my subjective views, plans, intentions and change the course of my life for better or worse" (Jung 1960: 525).

Likewise, in one of his last interviews Jung was asked if he believed in God. After a reflective pause, he replied, "I know. I don't need to believe. I know" (Jung 1977: 428). His response could well be considered a mystical one, thus validating charges by orthodox theologians that he was a mystic. However, their use of the term was a way to dismiss his experiential approach to religious realities as illegitimate. Unfortunately, mystic and mysticism remain suspect in theological circles or are reserved for a few select historical individuals.

Psychological mysticism expands the meanings of god, religion, and mystic and validates the universality of human experiences of the numinous. Those experiences are primary and ordinary; religious-naming, interpretation, and dogma are secondary and historically divisive.

Psychological mysticism cuts through centuries of dogmatic theology and speculation about external supernatural deities and devils. The mystical perspective is one of radical immanence.

TRAIL MARKER

I Know

Having taken leave of the
back porch of the Church
and my ancestral religious tribe
To scout out their possible futures
and my uncertain one
My scouting report is dire
reminiscent of the Old One
There is a new land just over the horizon
though not the one Promised
Giants nevertheless
Ancient psychic fears and prejudices
hidden beneath wishful god-talk
ignored for centuries
We must stare them down
eye to eye

the flesh-eating monsters
Standing in the path ahead
for our sacred species
and our holy humus.

Scouting reports to the faithful
evoke challenging questions about faith
Do you still believe in God
Have you lost your faith?

Carefully consulting my deep-down knowing
birthed from rock-solid conviction
revised by divine doubts
My response echoes Jung
facing the same question near his end
I do not need to believe
I know!

What did he know
that mystic
in psychological garb
What do I know
What do you know?

I know that I am
though I do not know
where I was before
nor where or how I will be after.

I know that life is full of mysteries
those we have named gods
no less so
That soul is as real as brain
the invisible as real as visible
That I am apprehended

by uncomprehended powers and presences
Who entangle me
in the net of unknowing.

I know that I am being sought
though I do not see my pursuers
nor clearly their intent
That I am also the one seeking
the seekers
A mutual game of hide and seek
forever playing out
in the meadows of my mind.

I know that faith and trust are twins
often confused with beliefs
that have other parentage
That beliefs breed mistrust of those
who believe differently
or not at all
That guarded beliefs
shrink the imaginative soul
While trust releases
the religious prisoners
That beliefs can change
and must
lest religious word-idols
slay us all.

I know that faith is delicate and hardy
like the first cry
announcing our arrival
on this spinning top
and our final sigh at the end
The trust of breath and gravity
being our first and last
faith-filled acts.

I know that we create our gods
from numinous experiences
not of our making
That we create gods
who in turn create us
and hopefully save us
from ourselves
That devils are created likewise
from dark shadowlands
projected onto the faces
of those we hate or fear.

I know that all religious dogma
is necessary subjective fiction
always needing a revised sequel
That all sacred texts are human words
about the gods we create
That our god-naming and religion-making
are necessary industries
to employ the human imagination.

I know that our visible Earth
is more precious
than a hoped-for heaven
That our at-one-ment with all
more precious than
atonement for a few
And if there is something like salvation
it will be for all
or none.

I know that I know very little
in the larger scheme of things
That I remain a final puzzle to myself
and others

Prompting the conclusion
to this trust-filled litany
But, then, what do I know
And you?

Journal: Through the lens of psychological mysticism, all of our thinking and imagining about gods, goddesses, and religion over the centuries are our subjective efforts to understand ourselves and our place in the mysterious cosmos. We are the meaning-seekers and meaning-makers. Furthermore, we are the god-makers in the sense that we give names to that which is ultimately unknown and unnamable, though we seem compelled to keep trying.

Psychologically, our deities and devils reveal much about the human psyche and its latent capacities for great good and great evil. They are projected images from our hidden depths, from the deep unconscious. In many respects, we have to see aspects of ourselves in projected forms before we can recognize them as our own. Psychological projection validates those mystical traditions that speak of *the god who dwells within you as you.*

In a further intuitive leap, Jung proposed that through these projective processes, the *inner god becomes aware of itself.* Thus, the mystery that we have named *God* needs human consciousness to become aware of itself.

Jung takes our intimate relation with divinity to its most mystical conclusion when he writes: "It was only quite late that we realized (or rather, are beginning to realize) that God is Reality itself and therefore—last but not least—man. This realization is a millennial process" (Jung 1969: 402; Wright 2018: 193).

Journal: We made religion into an effort to know God as an external being with personified human attributes. Then we had to understand

92

his gender, then his relationship to his only son, and to the notion of spirit. All of these were projected images onto a blank screen that we mistook for images of something external, rather than mirrors of our unknown selves. Once we engaged in complicated theological speculation, it has been difficult to undo.

Depth psychology provides a path to come home to ourselves, to our home in the natural world rather than a supernatural world populated with supernatural beings.

Journal: We do not honor spirit by becoming more spiritual but by becoming more human. This is the great paradox of incarnation, which remains a central Christian doctrine, yet poorly appreciated. The traditional Christian view supports spiritualization that takes one away from the Earth. Psychological mysticism promotes humanization and honors body/Earth/matter as a dwelling place for spirit. Jung addresses the mystical relationship between body and spirit when he writes: "The spirit is the life of the body seen from within, and the body the outward manifestation of the life of the spirit – the two being really one" (Jung 1924: 94).

Journal: The really meaningful aspects of life are not seized but surrendered to. Life happens to us more than we create it. For this reason, we speak of the *autonomy of the psyche*. For all our intellect and consciousness, every new moment is a step into the unknown, and every new stage as mysterious as the preceding one. Life (our best metaphor for god) is a continuous letting go in order to grab the next handhold, albeit always a slippery one.

In general, there are two possible attitudes toward this universal human dilemma—fear and trust. The latter constitutes a mystical attitude, yet not dependent on a particular religious belief or dogma or lack thereof. It does require paying attention. When referring to religion, Jung often used the Latin word *relegere,* an older derivation of *religion* that means to observe, to ponder, to take account of, or to attend all those things that cross our path (Jung 1960: 483). From a psychological mystical perspective, all things, invited or uninvited, are aspects of the sacred.

Journal: Soul (Psyche) can be imaged as the primary core of life itself, the animating energy of all things. As life's primary essence, soul has unlimited expressions or manifestations. We speak of the soul of the Earth and the soul of animals and, of course, the human soul. We employ soul as an adjective when we speak of soulful music or art or soulful places.

The primacy of soul elevates psychology (the study of soul) to an essential discipline. Although the human psyche is but one expression of soul, the human psyche is the *organic gateway* through which all life as we know it enters, and through which our particular life finds expression. Jung reminds us, "Without the psyche there would be neither knowledge or insight" (Jung 1965: 19).

The human psyche is the experiencer, the recorder, the interpreter, the decider, and the actor of all that happens. While this is an obvious fact, too often we have imagined the human soul as nothing more than an object to be saved for an afterlife.

All of our experiences are first of all psychological. Once we begin to name, interpret, and express an experience, it takes on other designations or names. This is why I propose that psychology precedes theology, and any other discipline or "ology." It is also why I propose that we create our deities and devils from experiences that we do not create.

TRAIL MARKER

Psyche/Soul

She a web of wisdom
known and yet-to-be known
Conscious and unconscious
The original
World Wide Web
With unlimited storage space
Never forgetting nor littering
Always recycling
Our mystical inheritance
and legacy
No password needed
except attention.

We are held together in Soul's web
Interconnected, interdependent, inter-are
and entangled
Colorful skeins
for the one tapestry
Archetypal patterns and potentials
emerging
from the depths.

We are children of the cosmos
Origin and parentage beyond knowing
Creator God and Evolution
two of many metaphors
to satisfy our curiosity
to name the unnamable
As Nature's meaning-seekers
and meaning-makers.

All matter
including matter considered dark
is alive and animated
A troupe of exotic
Soul dancers
in a long-running performance
inviting our participation
No wall flowers permitted
nor walls.

Soul remains her mystical name
for matters of the heart
While psyche speaks to the
scientific psychological mind
Heart and mind being
two sides of the same
cosmic coin
Kissing cousins to
spiritual and physical
Soul and body
forever wed.

Journal: A psychological mystic imagines the human psyche/soul as the organ of connection to, and relationship with, the one Reality, visible and invisible. It is also the organ of knowledge and insight about that Reality.

Theology begins with the notion of a preexisting, a priori, divine Being. Psychology begins with human experiences, some of which are designated religious.

Here, the waters of knowledge divide. I have been swimming in both streams for most of my adult life. They have converged in what I am calling psychological mysticism.

Journal: Unconscious religion, including unconscious Christianity, may be the most potent danger facing the human species and the Earth we inhabit. Even our nuclear weapons, as dangerous as they are, are at the mercy of the human psyche. As long as our gods are perceived to be remote beings beyond the natural world and separated from the human psyche, all manner of things are done in their name.

Jung's Analytical Psychology challenges us to bring our deities and devils home to the human psyche, where they originated and belong. They have been orphaned far too long.

Journal: Psychological consciousness is costly, but lack of it is deadly. Like my canine companion, Muffin, who shakes herself on awakening from her many naps, we have been shaking ourselves awake as a species for thousands of years. Yet, we so easily fall back to sleep, into unconsciousness. It seems so seductive, this comfortable lap, until the demands of growth, choice, and ethical living come calling. Then we discover our maturing muscles have atrophied and we have no strength for our primary task of wakeful living. Rumi implores, _don't go back to sleep._

Journal: Perhaps more than any person in the modern world, C. G. Jung was granted a far-reaching vision of the origins of the religious urge or instinct and, in turn, the psychological origins of all religions. This would include the creative and destructive powers that religions and religious persons hold in their hands, especially when religion and politics are wed.

To say it another way, Jung descended more deeply into the inner, invisible, mystical domain, stayed longer, and emerged to write more extensively about his experiences than any person to the present day. Yet, Jung remains relatively ignored by theological, psychological, political, and social leaders who are helping to shape the future of our species. On a more hopeful note, Jung's psychological theories continue to be revised and expanded, and more and more people on the margins of the disciplines mentioned above are finding meaningful sustenance.

Journal: The psychological mystical path is the most natural, most inclusive, and most satisfying religious way for the modern person. It does not require belief in a supernatural, theistic being that is separate from the natural world. It requires no complicated religious dogma or adherence to a set of ancient beliefs that were authoritative for ancestors. Psychological mysticism does not require the mediation of sacred experience by another person or authority or religious institution.

The primary invitation is to pay reverential attention to the mysteries that surround and infuse us moment by moment. Those mysteries meet us continually from both visible (so-called outer) and invisible (so-called inner) aspects of everyday life. They include all those experiences that the ego does not create, can't control, and cannot repeat on command.

The human ego is continually apprehended, i.e., approached, by that which it did not manufacture, that it may or may not comprehend, and yet to which it feels compelled to respond. The unsolicited experiences may approach from the visible or invisible, in solitude or in community, and during the day or night. The mystical presences may be embodied in another human, in Nature, or in a wide range of emotions that envelope one's body.

Responses to the mysteries that surround and infuse us range from delight to dread, from awe to disinterest, from ecstasy to terror, from intense curiosity to apathy, or from a desire to move toward or to retreat. Even denial or repression of an experience denotes a response.

To honor with reverential attention the mysteries that approach us unbidden constitutes a religious attitude in Jung's psychological framework. Such an attitude also describes a psychological mystic.

Journal: The primary concerns of psychological mysticism are *relationships*, rather than *redemption*. This includes relationship with our bodies and our psychological depths, relationship with the mysterious Cosmos and Earth of which we are an organic part, and relationship with all others with whom we are intrinsically linked.

The focus on relationships replaces the focus on redemption that has been the primary concern of Christian theology before and after the Reformation and Counter-Reformation. Matthew Fox notes that it was the redemption motif that fueled the religious invasions and destruction of indigenous peoples in Africa, in the Americas, and in the Pacific Islands. Such barbarisms were given credence by three notorious papal bulls of the 15th century that were known as the "Doctrine of Discovery." Those unfortunate religious pronouncements essentially viewed people and lands as property to be brought into the Christian fold at whatever the costs, and the costs were very high. We continue to reap the horrible harvest of such "redemptive" efforts. Elsewhere I have referred to such religious pathology as Monotheistic Madness.

Journal: With that mystical capacity called consciousness, humans have direct access to an apparently endless reservoir of cosmic memory referenced psychologically as the collective unconscious. It is the original internet, the interweb of life itself. Unlike so-called revealed religions, neither belief in an external deity nor a supernatural or human mediator is required to access the contents of the reservoir.

Connection is free, and there is no monthly fee, except wonder and awe and paying careful attention to all aspects of life itself.

Because of the fecundity of the unconscious, the Mystical Way has innumerable pathways, some of which may be identified as religious. Psychological mysticism pitches a large tent under which all those who have a passion for life and compassion for all find shelter and support.

Journal: In the analytical psychological myth or paradigm, the psychological Self can be seen as a substitute for the theological metaphor God, even though there are substantial theoretical differences. Both Self and God are metaphors for that which can be experienced, yet never fully known. I favor Self, however, because of all the centuries of toxic crust that has accumulated around God. Self is more difficult to genderize, literalize, commercialize, and militarize. Self also feels more inclusive (universal), immanent, intimate, and relational than a remote deity that supposedly incarnated in a one-and-only historical person.

The Self is an inner sage, a reservoir of natural and human wisdom accumulated over millennia. With consciousness we can contribute to that reservoir for the next generations.

Journal: In efforts to distinguish between an ego that is healthy and one that is ego-centered, it has become popular to talk about the false self versus the real self. While such differentiations can be helpful, they can also promote unnecessary dualisms. Furthermore, the notion of a false self is a carryover from the notorious doctrine of original sin, wherein there is something amiss that must be saved or redeemed.

There are more helpful images and metaphors for the mystery of the self that we are. From a mystical perspective, I like to imagine the self as a conduit or aperture through which the multifaceted mysterious energies of life flow. When the self is imagined this way, its growth, development, and health can be monitored or evaluated by questions like: *Is it constricted or open? Does it seek to go with the flow of life or against it? Is it predominantly trusting or fearful? Is it concerned only with itself or does it experience its connection with the all? Over time, is it more passionate or less so? More hopeful or despairing? Over time is its embrace of differences greater or less so?*

Such an image preserves the organic unity of the self and its intrinsic value as an organ through which life manifests; it recognizes the gift and burden of individual choice.

The mystical poet Rumi provides a similar image of the unitary self that is multifaceted. He suggests that the human self is a guest house with new arrivals every morning—joy, depression, sorrow, shame, delight, etc. Invite each of them in, he counsels, "because each has been sent as a guide from beyond" (Barks 2006: 366). Rumi's image avoids the notion of a false self while preserving all feeling states as legitimately human.

Journal: Individuation is the longing for and search for the ego's place in the larger Whole, what Jung called the Self. The ego-Self axis is the relational tether between the one and the Whole. If we employ the word God, we immediately eliminate all who don't subscribe to a theistic worldview or to a particular version thereof.

The whole history of our species can be understood as the continuous process and struggle to stay connected to the Whole from which we emerged while claiming and living our separateness. Analytical Psychology refers to this as the ego-Self axis or relationship.

Journal: Walking the path of psychological mysticism requires no less trust in the mysterious currents of life and in its purposeful unfolding, yet requires far more responsibility for our human choices, actions, behaviors, and partnership. Old clichés like "leaving it up to God" or "the Devil made me do it" are no longer permitted.

Journal: Those who critique depth psychology, Jungian analysis, and dreamwork as selfish navel-gazing have likely never engaged in the difficult and meaningful work such disciplines entail. A related misconception involves equating the process of individuation with individualism. The two are actually opposites. Rather than separating oneself from others and the social concerns of the world, the individuation process takes one more deeply into all aspects and difficulties of human life. Jung says it succinctly: "Individuation does not shut one out from the world, but gathers the world to oneself" (Jung 1946: 226).

The process of psychological individuation, as well as any and all authentic religion, promotes the ever-widening compassionate embrace of all life, visible and invisible, outer and inner. If spiritual practices, whether deemed religious or psychological, divide one from others and from the natural world, it would be wise to abandon such practices. They would do more harm than good.

Compassion for others is born from an interior place, from one's own hurts and wounds. Compassion requires intimate acquaintance with one's own humanity (not spirituality!) in all its glory and gore. It cannot be taught as an intellectual topic. We can teach people to be kind, even generous, but compassion comes from the embrace of our shadow, those parts of ourselves of which we are ashamed, those parts of ourselves we have judged to be inferior, and from those parts we wish to exclude from our persona. Compassion for another looks beneath the persona of the other and looks to the common core of humanity. Indeed, we are mirrors for each other.

Journal: Psychological mysticism takes one deeper into life, into the natural world, rather than lifting one out of life and away from the Earth. It is a state of *descendence* as compared to *transcendence* that is most often associated with religious mysticism. The goal is to be a full participant in ordinary, natural life rather than to achieve a supernatural existence, either before or after death. Psychological mysticism promises meaningful participation in the mysteries of life rather than easy answers to life's puzzles.

The goal of following a mystical path is not happiness or a state of bliss. Contentment would be a more accurate designation. Contentment suggests the capacity to engage life as it is, in its inevitable mixture, without withdrawal into self-pity, bitterness, or resignation. Equally, it means to be free to celebrate life's joys, ecstasies, and windfalls without hesitation or neurotic guilt. Contentment avoids the state of psychological inflation that accompanies narcissism and the state of psychological deflation that comes with victimhood. None of us is as good and holy as we imagine, or as bad and unredeemable as we fear. Contentment allows us to pitch our tent at a psychological sea level.

Journal: It is my experience that a Jungian psychological perspective has added depth and breadth not only to my religious/spiritual understandings, but to my life in general. It has enabled me, even forced me, to see the mystical significance of all life, global and cosmic, as well as my little piece of it. I must add, however, that my immersion in Analytical Psychology has not made my life easier, or provided easier answers to the questions and conflicts that are presented daily. In many respects, I am often even more conflicted, forced as I am to acknowledge the internal poles of the conflict at hand.

Speaking of the inherent conflicts in being human, and drawing on the Christian myth, Jung writes: "Man must now find ways and means to unite the divine opposites in himself. He is summoned and can no longer leave his sorrows to somebody else, not even to Christ because it was Christ who has left him with the almost impossible task of his cross. Christ has shown how everybody will be crucified upon his destiny, i.e., upon his self, as he was. He did not carry his cross and suffer crucifixion so that we could escape" (Jung 1958: 734).

Here, Jung uses Christ in its mystical sense rather than as a last name for Jesus. (See Wright, *Reimagining God and Religion*, Chapters 6-7 for an in-depth exploration of this vital distinction.)

Journal: Though the pursuit of a new or emerging religious paradigm is currently receiving abundant attention in progressive theological circles and producing a wealth of books, Jung's seminal contribution to this endeavor most often goes unacknowledged or barely mentioned. Much of what creative theologians are now proposing, the psychiatrist Carl Jung was writing about a half-century before.

While appreciative of Christian symbols, he was clear that Christianity was neither a complete nor a final religious myth. He proposed that future religions and their myths would require the discoveries of depth psychology if they were to be resources for the modern mind and ancient soul.

Jungian analyst and author Edward Edinger credits Jung with being among the first notables to identify in depth the imperative for a life-giving myth by which to live, and the problems generated when a former myth, like the Christian one, loses its vitality. This recognition grew out of Jung's awareness that he, like modern Western culture, suffered from the absence of an orienting and sustaining myth by which to navigate life. (See Edinger, *The New God-Image*, 1996.)

Jung's psychological myth, sometimes referred to as *a myth of consciousness*, prizes the expansion of psychological consciousness in general and religious consciousness in particular. These can be considered the twin goals of the individuation process. More than mere awareness or information, consciousness implies the capacity to integrate the ever-expanding knowledge of the interrelated, interdependent web of being of which we are a vital part, and the responsible embodiment or incarnation of that mystical perspective. It is the psychic capacity to apply one's experience of the external (visible) world to one's internal (invisible) world, and vice versa.

Journal: From the depth psychological perspective, the primary standard to evaluate the legitimacy of any religion or spiritual perspective is whether or not it promotes the expansion of consciousness in general and religious consciousness in particular. Does it promote the awareness of the creative and destructive capacities of the human person? Does it promote the self-understanding of its members? Does it address the mystery of who we are in relationship to the mysteries of the cosmos? Does it support the connection and interconnection of all there is—the human and more than human? Does it build bridges between and among all, or create divisions?

Journal: The mystical path leads to an experiential appreciation of our unity with all things visible and invisible, a unity that also preserves our individuality. So intimate is one's connection with all that is, he or she can say: *Although I am not you, neither am I other than you; although I am not the Earth, neither am I other than the Earth; and when I look at the night sky with its billions of stars, although I am not the stars, neither am I other than the stars.*

Furthermore, on the psychological mystical path, one discovers the most mysterious, and the most humbling, aspect of the divine/ human relationship: *Although I am not the Mystery at the heart of matter that we have named god, goddess, and God, neither am I other than that Mystery.*

Over the centuries, this most mysterious relationship has been addressed by many others. Jesus of Nazareth could say *I and the Father am one.* Meister Eckhardt could declare *My isness is God.*

Journal: This is the great mystical secret: *We are already one with the All.* We don't have to grit our teeth and work to make that happen. We are invited to trust what is and to live responsibly *as if* this is our nature and destiny.

All of this means that Life will win out. It will continue its faithful and forceful unfolding as it has been doing for billions of years, for what we call eternity. With the gift of mystical consciousness, we are privileged to participate in that unfolding as co-creators. We can also neglect that privilege, to our detriment, yet Life will continue its mysterious flow.

Journal: Some have supposed that we no longer have a myth by which to live, that we are a mythless culture. This is far from accurate. We always live by a set of values and a worldview that seeks to locate us in the larger scheme of things. Yet most often those values and worldview are unconscious and unexamined.

A case can be made that the myth that guides and drives modern Western religion and culture grows out of two delusions that we refuse to face: *There is some external divine source that will save us, either now or later; and if we just keep consuming more and more, we will be fine.* This unconscious cultural myth has its roots in monotheistic religion and thus has the force and power of the gods. If left unexamined, we will continue our mad rush toward extinction.

TRAIL MARKER

The Road to the City of More

Consult any western atlas or GPS
(Or simply ask Siri)
For directions to the City of More
A superhighway with soul left languishing
In two miles of ditches
For every mile of asphalt
Ditches filled with tear-stained adult toys
Touted by consumer priests
As missing pieces
To the happiness puzzles
Of vulnerable love-longing
Love-lonely humans.

Surely more is always better
Along with bigger and higher
And being great again.

How dare that mystical rabbi
Propose otherwise
That less is more
The first shall be last
And vice versa
That the greatest are servants of all?

What was that homeless
Itinerant mystic smoking
Declaring happy are the humble
Poor in spirit peacemakers?

What did he know
He who had only twelve followers
On his Twitter account?

Is the rapidly expanding City of More
A shining light to the nations
Or a flickering diminishing candle
On the edge of darkness?

Is the City of More
A beacon for freedom and justice
And equality for all
Or only for the well-connected
Who can afford health care?

Is the City of More
Capitalism's success
Or cannibalism's delight
Earth's honor or soul's sorrow?

Each of us is a
Judge and jury of one
Considering our verdict
In the City of More.

Now in the season of COVID-19
The highways to the City of More
Are less traveled
Except for the virtual ones
The skies are bluer
The air is cleaner
The birds seem to be rejoicing
While we ponder possible meanings.

Might it be that the expansion of
Soul
Requires less and less
And fewer and fewer
More subtraction than addition?

Journal: I share Carl Jung's chief concern that we no longer have a living myth that honors the invisible world and the necessity of our ongoing relationship with it. We have assigned the invisible half of Reality to external deities, devils, and angels while we content our suffering selves with that which is visible and rational.

Analytical Psychology was birthed, I think, to help us recover our connection to, and relationship with, the invisible aspect of Reality and to deepen our relationships with the visible aspects. It provides both language and disciplines to honor life in its visible and invisible wholeness.

When we are most alive and vital, we live on the threshold between the visible and invisible, and we move back and forth as necessary. Each night we receive glimpses of what is on the other side of the veil between the two. During the day, as well, the invisible manifests in the events and relationships that we experience. Analytical Psychology teaches us how to pay attention to the outside and inside, the above and beneath, the visible and invisible, and the beautiful and ugly of all that we encounter. Such careful, responsive attention constitutes a religious or mystical attitude toward life.

Journal: Drawing on the biblical creation myth, we are the Eighth Day of Creation. Each of us—you and I—has been given the capacity to continue the creation or destroy it. As a species we have yet to decide which of the two will be our legacy. With our daily decisions we are voting to be a co-creator or a co-destroyer. Human consciousness and imagination are both great gift and great burden. The burden is simply the rent we pay for being alive and sharing our beautiful nest. The gift is the joy of sharing the creative endeavor begun long before we arrived. What greater mission can we imagine? What great powers have been entrusted to us!

Journal: Jung reminds us that the unconscious, as an aspect of Nature, is alive and responsive. He writes, "... in the psyche there is nothing that is just a dead relic. Everything is alive, and our upper story, consciousness, is continually influenced by its living and active foundations" (Jung 1927: 31-32). Furthermore, a relationship of mutuality and reciprocity exists between the upper story (consciousness) and the deep unconscious. The face we turn toward the unconscious is the face the unconscious turns toward us. The human psyche and Nature are bound in a paradoxical, mystical mutuality. Domination by either side, or resignation on the part of the ego, is not allowed.

What will it mean to bring depth psychological wisdom to our concerns about climate change, environmental sustainability, and so-called natural disasters and pandemics? Or, more personally, how do we honor the relationship of mutuality and reciprocity in how we care for our bodies, including the natural processes involved in aging?

Journal: With that mystical capacity now called psychological consciousness, we humans have direct access to an apparently endless reservoir of cosmic history and human memory that Jung designated as the collective unconscious. This metaphorical memory bank is the original internet, the natural World Wide Web. It also has the imagined qualities that we have attributed to external divinities— omniscience (all knowing), and omnipresence (radically immanent). The human ego also experiences a third quality of the collective unconscious and its theoretical center, the Self, as being greater or more powerful (omnipotence).

Describing the collective unconscious, Jung writes, "… that unknown quantity in man which is as universal and wide as the world itself, which is in him by nature and cannot be acquired" (Jung, 1946: 312).

Journal: From the depth psychological perspective, all of our thinking, imagining, and writing about gods, goddesses, and religions over the centuries are subjective efforts to understand ourselves and our place in the cosmos. All theology is an outgrowth of psychological self-understanding, or lack thereof. The mysteries we have assigned to deities and devils mirror the mystery we are to ourselves as we experience the numinous natural world. That world is also our own flesh and blood. She is our Mother. Furthermore, the more we learn about the natural world through the hard and soft sciences, the more we learn about who we are and what role we may play in the great drama in which we find ourselves.

Unfortunately, we now speak reflexively of God as some *a priori* theistic being or entity rather than a name we have assigned to our unknown selves and our unacknowledged potentials. Our psychological mystical task is to come home to ourselves, and to reclaim both the creative and destructive capacities we erroneously exported to external deities and devils. Only then will we be able to exercise those capacities responsibly. Only then will our species survive and thrive.

Journal: Just now I had to apologize to our little four-legged companion, Muffin. She was looking out the glass door and the light was just right so that she saw her reflection. As she moved, her shadow moved, and she began barking with all the ferociousness

111

of her 18-pound body. She was sure that some intruder was lurking; after all, she is our homeland security agent!

I stood there laughing at her. That is, until I suddenly remembered that I/we do the same thing. We bark at people in the outer world who are dim shadows of our interior world!

So, I apologized to her, and she accepted my apology and returned to her sleep as if it was no big deal. Meanwhile, I reached for my journal to have a conversation with my shadow.

Journal: Each of us is a savior and a destroyer. Until we accept those contradictions and live a conscious crucifixion, we will crucify each other and our Earth home. The whole of the human enterprise is this: It is an experiment to accept both our angelic and demonic nature, individually and collectively, and to live responsibly our social contract assigned by Nature. Our major religions remain committed to external, theistic gods and the splitting of opposites. They keep aiding and abetting our inner destroyer while waiting for an external intervenor and savior. Our daily news, therefore, is a voyeuristic viewing of what is going on in our individual and collective hearts or psyches.

Our salvation begins when we abandon the notion that it will come from beyond, and when we free ourselves from the religious delusions of our own making. We have lived with those delusions far too long. We must save ourselves, if salvation is still possible. It may be too late. It is possible that the light of consciousness will remain lost in the black hole of our species, where light can escape no longer.

We are watching our inner darkness playing out on our streets, in the halls of Congress, and in wars and simmering global conflicts. It is in the darkness of our inner selves where the battles are waging and where they will be won or lost.

It may be that Analytical Psychology was birthed to rescue us from delusional religion and escapist theology. If so, it can only point us toward the source of our salvation. We have to access the courage to engage the twin tasks of expanding our consciousness and our compassion.

Journal: Individuation, the goal of depth psychology, is to become more fully ourselves, more fully human. Too often the religious or spiritual goal is to become something we are not. When religions are designed to promote our being something we are not, they lead either to feeling more than we are or less than we are. In the first case, the result will likely be self-righteousness or psychological inflation; in the latter, the result will likely be neurotic guilt, devaluation of self, and chronic depression, conditions sometimes referred to as a negative inflation.

To be fully human means to own our capacities for great good and great evil and to bear the gift and burden of choice about which to incarnate.

Journal: Murray Stein offers a succinct summary of a psychological myth for the modern person that goes beyond adherence to traditional religious dogma and creeds: "Follow your own personal myth as you discover it in your experience of the psyche and never mind if it conforms to public opinion, to collective religious teachings received in your tradition or to generally accepted cultural patterns. This journey will be your greatest treasure in life, possibly your greatest burden and suffering, but it will carry you to your individuation goal" (Stein 2017: 214).

Journal: Looking at our current political chaos through a depth psychological lens, Carl Jung's perspective on mob psychology seems apropos. In a mob or cult, the group consciousness is reduced to the lowest level of its least conscious members and its most influential leader. Individual consciousness and individual responsibility of mob members are given over to the mob leader.

President Donald Trump is a mob boss ruling over a political mob caught in mob psychology. Whatever he says is regarded as true, regardless of facts or consequences. Reflective thinking is not permitted. He demands absolute loyalty. One leaves the mob on the fear of public shaming or political death at the hands of the leader or other mob members. As Jung once noted, "People will do anything, no matter how absurd, in order to avoid facing their own souls" (Jung 1953: 99-101).

Trump has become such an international figure that he will be remembered not only as the 45th United States president, but as a divisive, destructive, death-dealing mythological figure. The Trump Complex may well become part of our psychological jargon.

I can be so psychologically scathing in my analysis because I was born and reared in a similar mob or cult—a religious one, evangelical Christianity. Furthermore, I promoted that cultish worldview for the first half of my life until choosing to separate myself from its toxic hold. The similarities of the political and religious mob are frightening.

For evangelical Christians, God is imaged as a remote boss who rewards good behavior and correct dogma by helping the faithful to win things like ballgames, political elections, and ultimately eternal life in heaven. Questioning the orthodox party line or, heaven forbid, leaving the cult, is rewarded with shunning in the short term and an assigned hot place for eternity in the long term.

According to evangelical Christians, the battle of Armageddon is fast approaching, when Jesus will return to gather the faithful, plus a few others who repent at the last minute. Since the end is near, there is no need to be concerned about climate change, racial and gender equality, or our rapacious use of Earth's resources. Such concern is set aside as fake news.

Of course, Donald Trump cares nothing about religion (evangelical or otherwise), or theology, or ethics. He will say or do anything to satisfy his lust for power, money, and adulation. He found an eager following among conservative Christians by promising to protect their religious worldview and values.

Journal: Supporting Donald Trump comes so easy for many, while critiquing him has become a favorite pastime for many others. However, if he is to be more than another scapegoat, it will require each and all of us to look into the mirror. Jung reminds us that _what we refuse to face inside meets us from the outside as fate._ Therefore, collectively and politically, we may have indeed constellated or invited our fate. We got what we asked for, albeit unconsciously so!

Trump supporters found a blond savior to _idealize._ Trump critics found a scapegoat to _demonize._ Both idealization and demonization are psychological projective phenomena, the purpose of which is to alert one to unconscious contents desiring to be owned and integrated into the personality. Both liberals and conservatives, or Trump critics and supporters, feel justified in their perspectives. Such justifications are usually accompanied by intense emotion felt in the body. When intense emotion and a bodily response coincide, we can suspect that psychological projections are at work. They are also indications of a numinous experience.

For centuries we have exported our deities and devils to realms beyond the physical domain, to a metaphysical heaven or hell. Such a theological and psychological exportation has left huge internal voids that are filled up with people, things, and causes that we idealize and demonize. These become our gods, and our service to them our truest religions.

The divisions related to Trump, along with a deadly pandemic that has become politically divisive, may well be the fate we invited by refusing to face and to own our inner deities and devils. If so, it may also be the latest attempt by the unconscious to get our individual and collective attention.

Journal: We are experiencing a "dark night of our collective soul." However, in the words of Jungian analyst Clarissa Pinkola Estes, "Do not lose heart, we were made for these times …" (See website: www. clarisapinkolaestes.com). We only need to take responsibility to do our one thing and to do it well. That is, we simply allow our own light to shine through the darkness, remembering that the outer darkness is a mirror of that darkness within. It may seem such a small or dim light in the thick enveloping darkness. Yet, it is all that is asked of us, *for we are the openings through which the light of consciousness enters the world.*

Remember, the experience of the sacred, or divine, or numinous is often preceded by a darkening, a depression, or a Dark Night of the Soul. The purpose, it seems, is to drive us deeper into soul.

Journal: I do become afraid of what could or might happen to us as a nation, world, or species. I am concerned about the possibility of more immediate suffering, and even the possibility of extinction.

But my greater existential fear is that I might lose my capacity to care or to give a damn. I fear my capacity to give up and become bitter and revengeful and to spend my remaining days in despair, depression, becoming a blob simply creating more carbon. This is my greater fear, my real terror.

I have already given up on traditional religion and its outdated myth, dogma, and institutions. I have retired from placing my hope in supernatural monotheism, including popular Christianity, as a path to peace and soul-making. I am no longer willing to splash around in the religious shallows in order to be seen as a member of the tribe, or even religiously/spiritually sane. That kind of reputation is no longer appealing.

So, my greatest fear is that I might give up. The recurring temptation is to regress, to reach back for old handholds and old security blankets. Yet, the turnstile at the exit of traditional religion turns only one way. There is no going back. One needs to be careful, therefore, of taking leave of places seemingly secure, yet shallow, for the risky possibility of something more meaningful. The invisible sign at the entrance to the mystical path reads something like: *Hungry seekers beware. Enter at your own risk!*

So far, the courage to continue has presented itself when my need has been greatest. I am sustained by the mystical knowing that what I seek was seeking me before I began.

TRAIL MARKER

Why?

Why have we spent centuries
building religious highways to heaven
When Nature's numinous paths
lead directly Home?

Why must we look for miracles
from external supernatural deities
When Nature's internal miracles
are super enough?

Why do we invest
in the industries of remote deities
to save us
Rather than investing in
honest self-reflection
to save ourselves from ourselves?

Why do we consider
walking on water
or changing water into wine
More miraculous

than our next breath
that repeats its miracle
fifteen to twenty times
every minute?

Why do we continue to spill blood
in the name of the one
whose spilled blood
was supposedly spilled for all
And why are we so enamored
with drinking symbolic blood
more than ridding our world
of blood-spilling weapons?

Why do we continue to elevate
beliefs over trust
creed over character
skin color over soul
men over women
masculine over feminine
miracles over mystery
and Bronze-age men
and their books
over common sense?

Why is sex considered so dirty
so shameful
when each of us is its joyful
outcome?

Why do we fight so tenaciously
for our babies in the womb
Yet so eagerly send our babies
to fight and kill other babies
Who happen to be born

from wombs of the same flesh
but with different names?

Why does it take a lifetime
to come home to ourselves
When we live so close?

And the most puzzling question of all
why do I suppose
(why do we suppose)
I see more clearly than most
the important issues
facing our world
and our species?

CHAPTER FOUR

DREAMS ALONG THE MYSTICAL PATH

Dreams may be the clearest validation that we live in a mysterious, mystical cosmos. They also validate that we are continually being sought out and addressed by those mysteries, by whatever name we know them.

In my previous book *Reimagining God and Religion,* dreams are imaged as "Strangers in the Night," strangers who bear nightly gifts for our psychological balance and health. Readers who desire a comprehensive review of dreams and dreamwork may find that essay helpful (Wright 2018: 149ff).

As indicated in the introduction to this book, I am including dreams from my own journals since dreams are such a vital resource on the mystical path. In my psychological usage of mystic and mystical described in Chapter Two and throughout this volume, every dream is a mystical gift. Dreams come unbidden from the mysterious depths and are unmediated except by the dreamer's ego on awakening. Their purpose is to strengthen the connective tissue between the ego (the center of consciousness) and the Self, the metaphor for the centering, balancing, reconciling energy of the total psyche, conscious and unconscious. Or, in more poetic language, dreams are ways the Self woos or courts the ego for intimate relationship. The intensity of the Self's mystical courtship is captured by the Sufi mystic and poet Hafiz: *I have fallen in love with someone / who is hiding inside you / we should talk about this problem / otherwise I will never leave you alone* (Ladinsky 2002:175; Wright 2018: 153).

Dreams prefer the language of symbols, images, and metaphors; they are rarely literal. They most often serve a compensatory function to one's current conscious attitude, thus assisting the dreamer to live at a metaphorical sea level, or to follow the mystical Middle Way, or to make one's way through a labyrinth of opposites that is life itself.

From the many recorded dreams in my personal journals, I have selected some that include common or universal images, motifs, and patterns of human thought, behavior, and predicaments (i.e., archetypal). Most often the dreams address one or both sides of universal opposites—Life/Death, Body/Soul, Masculine/Feminine, Individual/Collective, Lost/Found, Light/Shadow, Order/Chaos, Ever Ancient/Ever New, Trust/Fear—to mention a few of our common psychic building blocks.

The dreams are offered without personal context, comment, or associations. While they may provide glimpses into my own psychological life and individuation process, their main value will be the degree to which the reader allows the dream images and symbols to draw up from within his/her own depths that which is seeking light. For this purpose, it may be helpful to own and internalize the dream, as if it were your own, beginning with the phrase, "In my dream." With your personal journal in hand, record personal associations, emotions, memories, and amplifications that are drawn up from within; then carry the dream images around like a magnet to see what gets attracted to them from the daytime world.

These suggestions are similar to the invitation in the introduction to read magnetically. Magnetic reading means to allow the words on the page to draw up within the reader his/her own words, images, and meanings. Images and symbols in dreams are especially conducive for this kind of engagement since they come from a universal storehouse. Whether the images and symbols are from our own dreams, or borrowed and internalized from the dreams of another, or found in the news of the day, they can be powerful subjects seeking relationship. Again, psyche meets us from within and from without; psyche has no geographical boundaries.

The relational aspects of dreams and dreamwork may be summed up in a phrase attributed to Jung: *It is not _understanding_ our dreams that brings about transformation, but the intensity with which we engage the images.* In his journal named *The Red Book*, Carl Jung reveals in word and image what intense engagement means. And while our dream journals will likely not be as beautiful and grand as his, our labors will be equally honored by the unconscious, which desires and needs our consciousness. Consciousness is our light to illumine the darkness of mere being (Jung 1965: 326; Wright 2018: 56).

In speaking and writing about dreams, Carl Jung often drew on poetic and mystical language. For example:

> The dream is a little hidden door in the innermost and most secret recesses of the soul, opening into that cosmic night which was psyche long before there was any ego-consciousness, and which will remain psyche no matter how far ego-consciousness extends (Jung 1933: 144-45). ... In each of us there is another whom we do not know. He speaks to us in dreams and tells us how differently he sees us from the ways we see ourselves (Jung 1933: 153). ... The whole dream-work is essentially subjective, and a dream is a theatre in which the dreamer is himself the scene, the player, the prompter, the producer, the author, the public, and the critic ... all the figures in the dream (are) personified features of the dreamer's personality (Jung 1960: 266).

So, with journal in hand, you are invited to own and internalize the following dreams and dream images as your own. May they open up hidden doorways into your own inner world, and may you find aspects of yourself therein.

Journal: (Dream) A man is showing me how to dig a tunnel; he is an archaeologist type. There is a tunnel already dug on the other side, and he is illustrating how to dig down through the center and connect with the deep tunnel. He is using a small model in the living room, and my wife, Kay, is there off to the side.

As he is digging, he says the soil is 200,000 or 600,000 years old; there are different levels, different ages. Actually, the tunnels are from both ends, and he/we are digging through the center to connect the two. I call Kay over to show her how fascinating it is.

Journal: (Dream) A tiny baby form is convulsing, and I go over to help. It looks like a cross between a small newly born human and a bird, with mouth/beak wide open, convulsing. I take a look, can't see its tongue, and say, "The most important thing is its breath. We need to get help because I nor anyone here knows what to do. Follow me."

I begin walking and screaming for help from someone who knows about convulsions. Two Black men up on a hill with headphones raise their hands, and I motion for them to come and help. One moves toward the infant, and I keep screaming for help.

Then I turn around, and the young man is returning to the place on the hill. I go over and ask someone how things are with the infant, and the person tells me that the man performed the procedure/maneuver and the baby resumed breathing. I say that I need to learn the procedure for future crises.

Journal: (Dream) A dead body is found in a small room/closet space. Later, it is determined that his penis has been cut off and the authorities say they will wait for daylight to search for the penis in the nearby woods.

Another penis image a few nights ago: I am with three women, naked, and I have a huge erection, and one woman is ready/willing for intercourse. As I approach her, I pause with the thought, "I can do this, but should I?" I withdraw from entering her.

Journal: (Dream) I am involved in a worship service. I am like an advisor, not fully in charge, yet responsible. Each of the young people is given a passage of Scripture to talk about spontaneously.

The service begins. I am first, and my Scripture passage is *Love one another as God has loved you.* I get up and start to say something. I'm trying to remember a story or an example to use. As I am talking, a couple begins to cause a disturbance. The woman is complaining that no one furnished a wheelchair for her, and they get up and stalk out. There is general disturbance and talking, and I keep trying to talk over it to no avail.

My time is up, and I am still scrambling to say something—for after all, I am one of the responsible ones. I blurt out that what has just happened is the clearest example of the Scripture passage—a living example right before us. The woman had a need and was ignored. Someone says they tried but she did not cooperate.

I say with insistence that the Scripture passage is impossible to live. We can't love others as God loves us because we do not have the power. And I walk off while a second speaker is coming forward.

I go off at some distance and watch the chaos. At one point I am on a bus with my feet propped up as if I want nothing to do with what is happening. I see more and more people leaving the church. Apparently, they can't take any more of the silliness.

Journal: (Dream) I have arrived on Iona with a new pilgrimage group, and nothing is the same as before. There are new buildings and construction. There are no familiar landmarks.

The group is rowdy, complaining. They won't listen as I attempt to orient them. And it is raining furiously, and I have forgotten my umbrella.

I tell them to go to lunch and how to get there, but it turns out that the dining hall is far away. I tell them we will gather again at 2 p.m. Then I remember that I did not bring my Celtic notes. I have no idea what I will teach or do. I am the only leader.

Now some have already returned from lunch. They say it was awful, same old slop. I go to the dining hall and I don't recognize the food on my plate.

Then I return to my dorm/room, and there are people sleeping in the hallways on the floor. I find my room, number 23 or number 22. I go in, and it is in disarray.

The rain has stopped, and the sun is peeking out, and I think that is a good sign.

Journal: (Dream) Someone has gifted me with a horse that is to be born soon. I drive out into the country looking for a pregnant horse. I ask someone if they have seen a pregnant horse, and they say no.

Then I see a man who looks like a farmer and I approach him. When I ask him about a pregnant horse, he is both surprised and a little disappointed because he had thought that no one would claim the foal-to-be and he would have it.

He asks me how I would care for the baby horse, and I tell him I don't know. Maybe I can rent a place or build a fence. I don't have a clue. Then he gives me a piece of meat-looking substance for an initial meal, as if he wants the best for the foal.

I ask him/them how long the gestation period for horses is, and they say they don't know. However, the farmer says that the horse was conceived on Super Bowl day, and his wife agrees. There is a suggestion that they remember having sex that day. The birth is to happen soon, although they do not know the exact day.

Meanwhile, I am having images of keeping the horse on my porch or somewhere until I can figure out what to do.

(I look back in my journal to see what may have been conceived on Super Bowl Sunday. I was writing about soul, and the fact that we create our deities and devils from experiences that we don't create. I was also remembering my immaturity when I promoted the "Four Spiritual Laws," and I wrote: *It may be an act of grace that we don't live long enough for all our so-called truth to be revealed as delusions—that is what children and grandchildren are for!*

I had also apologized to Muffin for laughing at her for barking at her shadow in the glass door leading to the back porch. I confessed to her that I do the same thing.)

Journal: (Dream) I am taking a final exam for a course taught by my college baseball coach. He has laid out the exam questions in several different stacks, and members of the class have gone in and selected their questions. Many have already completed the exam and are sitting around chatting and socializing.

I seem to be one of the last to finish and I try to find a place to sit and write. But there are too many distractions, and I also learn that I have not picked up one part of the exam questions.

One part of the exam is about the environment. I remember that we had some lessons on that, but I don't have my notes, or I can't remember, but I figure I know enough to respond.

I am feeling stressed, lagging behind, frustrated that I can't find a quiet desk to concentrate on the exam. I remember that Coach was not the best teacher, yet he knew his stuff and designed creative exams.

In another part of the dream, I am lost, wandering, trying to find my way to the baseball game and our team. At one point, I say we need to go in a certain direction, toward the tall lights that surround the athletic fields, but another leader says we need to go the other way. We keep wandering. I need to go to the bathroom, but the stalls are either crowded or filthy.

I finally go in the direction I had suggested earlier and I arrive at the game, which is already underway. I approach my coach, and he immediately begins to substitute us for the players who were fill-ins.

Journal: (Dream) All night I see multiple bodies that are dismembered, body parts everywhere, with blood and gore, and feelings of horror and disgust. I keep waking up horrified and wondering if the dismembered images are purposeful for reform or reconstituting. Then I return to sleep with more blood and gore. I wake up exhausted.

Journal: (Dream) I am in a new house that seems poorly arranged, too small, and not well furnished. The den is sunken and dark. I ask about some furniture and my favorite chair. Kay says she gave them away when we moved. The house is not homey as before; stale, stark, dark, not inviting.

Journal: (Dream) I am at a conference, and the leader is a very beautiful, vivacious, intelligent woman. Her topic is death and mourning. She asks me about the second stage of grief, and I say "anxiety and stress," but that is not the right answer.

At the end of the lecture, she comes among the group looking for someone to walk with, and she chooses me. It's both gratifying and embarrassing given I have spent time with a couple of other women. I look around for one of them, but she has already left the conference early.

The leader and I walk and talk like good friends and potential romance, and we keep choosing to walk in the light/sun rather than in the shadows.

Journal: (Dream) I am traveling with a group and I go on ahead to see what is there. I come to a washed-out place in the road, a wide gully, not navigable by car, although there is one thin pattern of car/vehicle tracks. I return to the group and tell them, but they seem doubtful of my report. But when they arrive at the washed-out place, they see the problem; their low, sleek cars would get stuck.

Journal: (Dream) I am at a conference and talking with a professor-type woman. I am expounding on the relationship of matter and spirit, and I am making the case for matter being more important and more powerful. I am aware that what I am saying is not the common or orthodox view. The woman is expressing the opposite view to mine.

Meanwhile, I am eating a huge piece of chocolate candy, stuffing my mouth with it, and I am mildly aware that this seems out of place, but I continue.

We are talking about Jung's vision of the divine turd smashing the cathedral, or maybe I begin thinking about that vision to support my viewpoint. I keep working out in my mind the relationship between matter and spirit.

I conclude that it was the "matter within the spirit," i.e., God's shit that destroyed the cathedral, the cathedral being the symbol of contained divinity or spirit.

Journal: (Dream) I am suddenly cast in the role of a TV reporter, responsible for a newly begun festival. The TV reporters have all died or left. I can't find photos to use, but son Scott hands me several small ones.

The man in charge, who has practically forced me into the role, keeps running around trying to ready all the new reporters. At one point, he asks me what I think/feel about "cyber death"; I take that to mean some kind of threat to me/us/or the TV station. I tell him I don't know. I ask him what network the station is connected with, like CBS, and he says some other, unfamiliar network.

It's almost time to go on the air, and I am clueless about what I will say. The man clarifies that I am not responsible for sports scores, etc., only the festival. I ask how long the festival has been taking place, and he says this is the first of what will be an annual event.

I feel scared, bat-shit crazy, completely unprepared for the shaming and embarrassment soon to happen.

Journal: (Dream) Steve and Matthew, local plumbers, show up in our driveway/yard looking for a water main break. Apparently, someone has called them.

They discover that the break is not in our yard but on the side of our property where there is a natural stream. The water main break is right next to the stream, and they begin to gather their equipment to repair it.

Now, Kay is sitting and reading in the middle of the commotion and equipment, though now it's in our living area. I tell her she needs to move so she won't get hurt.

Journal: (Dream) A few others and I are lost in some ancient, medieval or postmodern city with buildings that are so tall they seem to disappear into the clouds. One arena-like area is filled with ancient chain-like structures, and we wonder together what this is used for. Though there are people everywhere, I do not remember seeing them, only the ancient/postmodern, futuristic structures.

We leave our hotel and now we can't find our way back. I can't remember the name of the hotel, nor can the others. My cell phone is almost dead. I suggest someone call the woman who guided us here, or sent us here, so she can remind us the name of the hotel. But the call does not go through.

I am actually searching for my car, which I had parked near the hotel, but I/we have no clue which direction to move among the tall structures.

We are lost, and I feel responsible as the supposed leader.

Journal: (Dream) I am at an event with James Hollis, who is teaching, and I am to follow him. I have no clue what I will say or teach. I have some notes, but they all seem useless and have no real themes. I run through my mind about possible themes or stories, but nothing seems to fit. Meanwhile, my fear grows, and the possible shame.

Hollis appears younger, and his talk seems to me uninteresting, although the others seem interested and laugh at his jokes. I can't think of anything I could say that would be funny.

Now, Hollis is almost finished, and my fears increase. I go looking for a bathroom but I can't find one, and the ones I have used before are closed or blocked. I walk around some familiar "dream places" but I can't find relief.

I wake up relieved and go to the bathroom to relieve.

Journal: (Dream) A young girl, plain and simply dressed, approaches. Before I know it, she has picked my pocket—my wallet, keys and some other special object. She refuses to give them back.

Meanwhile, another girl/woman approaches and asks me to protect her from some man who is harassing her. I agree to do so, although I neither see nor confront him.

Journal: (Dream) I am in a class being led/taught by a very conservative couple. At one point, I begin talking about some of my current concerns. One is the synchronicity of the psychic virus and the COVID-19 virus coming together at the same time. I make a point to say that God has not caused the situation, but it is a meaningful coincidence.

The other issue is about the word God. I say that five years ago no one was concerned about the word, but now many are concerned. I had checked my journals to confirm that.

After I finish talking, there is silence. No one speaks, and I ask if anyone has anything to say; there is still an uncomfortable silence. In my own discomfort, I begin to sing, "There is a kind of hush all over the world tonight." Still no response.

Journal: (Dream) Kay and I are attending a large Baptist church. My mother and father are with us but outside; they are delayed. Kay and I go in and are seated in a wing of the sanctuary, off to the left out of sight of the minister. Mom and Dad come in and are looking for us, and I get up to show them where we are.

Kay begins to talk loudly, though she thinks she is whispering. I think she is being rude and disruptive, and I shush her. I finally tell her that if she does it again, I will leave. It's embarrassing; I feel shame.

The minister comes over to us and begins to preach to me about the word *vestige*, and I don't know what the word means. I set him straight in a passive way; he doesn't know who I am. I feel superior to him and his supposed intellect. He recognizes Kay as someone he met and invited her to attend his church, and he is glad she has come.

I begin moralizing to him, saying that it is easy for him to get people to come to church but harder to keep them there. I tell him to be a good pastor. That is the most important thing.

The service is over, and my son sees a boat outside that he assumes belongs to the minister, and he tells me how roomy it is. He is enamored with it. Then, the minister and his son appear in their fishing outfits, and they seem happy and ready to go fishing after his work. The boat is not his, but they are being taken by some other means to their outing. He and his son seem happy and having fun. I remain angry.

Journal: (Dream, Night of Winter Solstice) I just dreamed that I have been chosen to die this year. We are seated in a large group. A familiar younger man is standing before us. He announces that if our name is called, to come forward. He is selecting those who have been chosen to die.

I am seated on the front row, confident that it is not yet my time. He looks out over the group, calls a man by his name, and asks him to come forward.

He then places his hands on my shoulder, and with some sadness, I think, calls me to come forward. I stand up and walk slowly with him and a growing number of others. I look back and see Kay crying, grief-stricken, reaching out to me with outstretched arms, but I turn and walk on.

I recognize many of the "chosen"—some are older, others younger. Some are in shock, some are crying, but none of us is resisting or running away. We are simply gathering as a group, having been chosen to die.

It is assumed that it will be this year, although it feels immanent since we are being separated from the others, from family and friends. It feels like it is happening in the moment.

In the dream, I had just tied my shoes to go across the street, where Kay is watching a neighbor's child or dog. Muffin is running back and forth across the street, and I need to get her and make her safe. The scene is the Arrowoods' house of my childhood, the home of Tillie Arrowood, who died in a car accident as a teen. It was my first experience of an untimely death.

Journal: (Dream) I am leading and teaching a large group of people in a conference/retreat setting. I have them under my attention, my spell. They trust me.

I decide to do an experiment: I place a gun/revolver in my waistband and display it discreetly, to see what the reaction/response will be. The people are alarmed and disappointed as if the presence of a gun discredits or undermines everything I have taught or stand for. I can see it in their eyes and feel it. They do not know it is a toy gun.

At the break, several pursue me to express their alarm, to question me, etc. Meanwhile, I plan to tell them about the experiment, but I don't want to spoil it yet.

Journal: I am teaching/instructing my son about important matters labeled "cornerstones." I have spent a lot of time on "multiple," a topic/ issue that seems important.

Now I am beginning with another important topic or cornerstone, "kindred." It's as if I am teaching him some foundational pieces of life and what really matters.

He is attentive, and I feel satisfied with my instruction.

Journal: (Dream) I am at a house next to the town where I am to preach this a.m. and I am trying to get ready. Daddy is there, and I'm waiting for him to get out of the bathroom so we can go to our house, where I need to change and dress for the church service in about an hour.

Another man is the *real* minister at the church, but I am the preacher for the morning.

I am trying to leave. Daddy finally gets his stuff together, and we walk out toward where the car is supposed to be.

Now Kay is having a crisis and needs my attention. She and our granddaughter are in the kitchen, and the lights go out. Our granddaughter is playing with some electronic gadgets and has caused a short circuit. Kay is helpless, already in the early stages of memory loss. I find the power box and flip the switch. The lights come on.

But now our granddaughter is playing inside a large microwave-type oven, and fire and flames are shooting out. She is unaware of the danger, so I tell her to get out. I am worried that she may put another little girl in danger.

But I have to leave. I am late. I can't decide if I need to take some clothes from this house or use the ones at the real house I am trying to reach.

Now I call for Muffin, who has wandered off, and she comes running finally, and we get off to find Daddy and the car. But they are nowhere to be found. A woman had parked the car the night before, and she had said it was near the First Baptist Church.

Now I am carrying Muffin. Another man, a slow-witted type, is with us, and we are looking for Daddy and the car. Meanwhile, it is now less than an hour before I am to be in the pulpit. I have a cell phone in my pocket but I don't know whom to call.

Then we come to a huge church that is laid out in a mandala fashion, or square, and we circle it, looking for the car. Muffin is getting heavy, so I put her down. Now we are in some crevices, still searching, feeling totally helpless and lost and unsure what to do. I wake up totally exhausted.

Journal: (Dream) I am supposed to preach somewhere, but I have forgotten where, and I don't know what I will preach about, and tomorrow is the day.

I think about many of my old illustrations and stories that I have used over the years, but nothing seems to fit. Then I remember an old illustration titled a "Fifth Grade Boy's Essay on Anatomy" that ends with: _And that's all there is, except what's inside, and I ain't seen that yet._

(End of Dreams)

I have decided to include the "Fifth Grade Boy's Essay on Anatomy," mentioned in the last dream. My reasons for doing so will be included in the reflections that follow:

A Fifth Grade Boy's Essay on Anatomy

Your head is kinda round and hard
and your brains are in it
and your hair on top of it.
Your face is in front of your head
and that's where you eat.
Your neck is what keeps your
head off your shoulders
which are sorta shelves
which you hook your overall straps on.
Your stomach is something
if you don't eat often enough
or too much
it hurts.
Your spine is a long bone in the back
that keeps you from folding up,
And your back is always behind you
no matter which way you go.
Your arms are to pitch with
and to reach for biscuits.

Your fingers stick out from your hands
so you can scratch and point.
Your legs are what you get to first base on.
Your feet are what you run on
and your toes are what you get stumped.
That's all there is
Except what's inside
And I ain't seen that yet.

<u>Reflections on Dream and Essay:</u> The dream might be considered one of those throw-away dreams, meaning one that the ego considers too short, too frivolous, or too inconsequential to warrant attention. I imagine each of us can identify with that attitude. I was tempted to exclude it in this chapter, along with the essay. At first, I thought it might be too lighthearted for such an important psychological subject as dreams and dreamwork.

On further reflection, however, with personal associations and archetypal amplifications, the dream began to reveal its treasures for me personally, and perhaps it might for you the reader as you internalize it.

After the dream, I searched my files for the lighthearted essay. I had not read it for many years, nor do I remember the name of the speaker from whom I borrowed it a half-lifetime ago. It was lost deep in a filing cabinet, much like contents of consciousness that disappear into the personal unconscious; or like dreams that fly away on awakening. Those contents never totally disappear, however; they get recycled by some mysterious inner artist, builder, writer, poet, or wisdom figure that we have named the psychological Self. Apparently, the Self decided it was time for recycling.

In the dream and essay, I am struck with the allusions to several pairs of opposites that these pages have sought to address—Outer/Inner; Body/Soul; Matter/Spirit; Visible/Invisible; Persona/Self. The dream seems to be a comment on my outer writing project, especially my sometimes obsessive attempts to find just the right words or phrases that will heal the world. Alas, all visible words fail to capture the invisible, the ineffable, and the mystical—*all that we ain't seen yet.* Equally important, the dream reminds me to trust the inner writing project under the direction of an invisible Author.

Widening the lens, the concluding phrase, *that's all there is, except what's inside, and I ain't seen that yet,* has fueled most of the creative endeavors of our species—all of our efforts to see the unseen, to peer behind the veil to catch glimpses of what eludes the naked eye. These endeavors would include much of our hard and soft sciences; much of our art, poetry, and music; all of our religions; and, yes, all of depth psychology, including Jung's Analytical Psychology. It is humbling to remember that we will be forever *groping in the dark.* Of course, the dark is the seedbed of trust.

Finally, the dream and essay remind me of our bodies, which are mysterious marvels and house so many other mysteries. Our bodies are the first responders to the approach of the numinous, the mystical visitors who cross the threshold night and day. Extending the image, our bodies are extensions of the body of the Earth, a body so beautiful and bountiful, visible and invisible.

That's all there is
Except what's inside
And I ain't seen that yet

(But let's keep trying!)

CHAPTER FIVE

WISDOM FOR THE MYSTICAL PATH

Journal: The Wisdom of the Universe is not stored up in a metaphysical domain and dispensed by a heavenly parent. Wisdom is within life itself, in the depths, within each of us, *in the innerness of all things* (Rilke). The human psyche/soul is wired to Nature's Wisdom, and it is our task and delight to make visible that Wisdom and to be that Wisdom.

The psychological word for the storehouse of Wisdom is the unconscious, in both its personal and collective aspects. The unconscious is also the womb where our future life is gestating and from which our future will be birthed. We are privileged to be the midwives and co-creators of the future. We can accept that role, or neglect it at our peril.

This journal entry, and many similar ones, gave birth to the following imaginative *email from Wisdom* addressed to those on a mystical path:

DATE: Past/Present/Future
FROM: Wisdom Within the Universe @ Human Heart.com
TO: Travelers on a Mystical Path
Subject: Notice of Change of Address and a Few Reminders

Dear Ones,

I know that these are terrifying times for you, as they are for me, so I send this heartfelt message using the latest technology that your species has created. You have been very clever, and I applaud you for that. Keep it up! Yet you have been slower to access the deep Wisdom available to you in order to use what you have created for your common good. We can do better, you and I. We must do better. Thus, the purpose of this message.

First, let me advise you of my new address. The notice of my new domain was sent out more than 400 years ago by Copernicus (1473-1543) and Galileo (1564-1642), yet apparently many of you did not take notice. I suppose it got lost in all the many things you have to keep up with. Believe me, I know how that is. I, too, have a lot to manage: the billions of galaxies, each with billions of suns called stars; black holes and gravity; keeping the Earth on its axis and your feet on the ground as the Earth spins at 1,000 miles per hour; managing the seasons and the twice-daily tides, which keep rising; reminding birds when and where to fly; and the art of photosynthesis, to name just a few. You know these things because it is your species that has named them all, even as you have named me, Wisdom Within the Universe. Thanks for that. You have done a great job with your naming. More about that in a moment.

Now, about my change of address. My old address was Supreme Judge *Outside* the Universe @ Heaven.com. Most of you were familiar with that old address. It was used for centuries. My new address is: Wisdom *Within* the Universe @ human heart.com.

Please make the changes in your address books. I will no longer be checking messages at the old address and I do desire to keep in touch, as I know you do. We need each other. You cannot do without me, nor I you. Partners we are. Co-creators of the future we are.

Now, a few words about my preferred new email name and address. Though I will still respond to all the names you have created for me over the tens of thousands of years—including gods, goddesses, spirit, Zeus, Logos, Eros, Sophia, Tao, the Mind of Christ, Buddha Mind, Greater Self, and more recently God, I actually delight when you create new names. I must say that the name God has lost most of its pizazz for me. So many things have been done using that name and under that flag—things not very wise and atrocities that have caused me great grief. That three-letter word has been so literalized, domesticized, commercialized, politicized, and militarized that, frankly, I cringe a little when I hear it. That name—God—was once a helpful name when you were little and young. But now that you have grown up, you may want to put it on the shelf for a few generations while it recovers from its overuse and abuse.

New names show me that your species continues one of your most creative gifts—that is, giving names to all things wherein I reside: all the flowers of the field, the trees, the aforementioned birds, and those planets and stars, and the Sun and Moon. And you have named all those arenas of knowledge about me: Cosmology, Biology, Anthropology, Neurology, Psychology, Theology, and more recently, Evolutionary Biology and Evolutionary Psychology. There is so much of me that you have discovered and honored, and so much more to come. Where would we be if your species had not undertaken your primary mission of seeing, of wondering, of beholding, of looking through telescopes and microscopes, and of naming what you have seen and experienced? Why, it would be as if nothing of me existed if you had not given witness! Keep it up. You haven't seen anything yet.

And, as I just mentioned, I delight in new names because I am so diverse and many-sided and multidimensional; I dread above all being boxed in or treated like an object or a possession. Though I honor your intent, I have never been comfortable with the phrases *Our God* or *My God*. It makes me feel like an object, a possession, rather than a subject for relationship; and relationship is my greatest desire, and your greatest need.

You can never have too many names for all my mysteries. I love it when your poets speak about me; for instance, when they let their imagination soar and say things about me like:

You are the future,
the red sky before sunrise
over the fields of time.

You are the cock's crow when night is done
You are the dew and the bells of matins,

141

maiden, stranger, mother, death.
You create yourself in ever-changing shapes
that rise from the stuff of our days -
unsung, unmourned, undescribed,
like a forest we never knew.

You are the deep innerness of all things,
the last word that can never be spoken.
(Barrows and Macy, 1996: 119)

Oh my! Rilke's words are music to my celestial ears! How I love your beautiful words! Just remember, words are your invention not mine. Enjoy them. Use them to unite not to divide, to build bridges, not walls. Don't weaponize them; they can be lethal. And do not <u>worship</u> the words you have created, especially your religious ones. Yes, I know you are inclined to attribute your religious words and sacred texts to me to give them more supposed authority and power, to compete with other religious or political tribes, and to win unnecessary and unwinnable religious arguments. That is not helpful or very wise. It has caused too much grief for too many years. All words are like the flowers of the field that bloom beautifully, then wither and die, and return to the Earth to serve as fertilizer for the next season or the next generation.

So please use your beautiful, sensitive *bodies*, your sharp *minds*, and your rich *imaginations* to come up with a better way to partner with me in co-creating the future. Access Wisdom, which you have inherited as an organic part of the natural world. The natural world has stored my Wisdom for the ages. You are rooted in that Wisdom, as beautiful, strong trees are rooted in the Earth from which you, too, sprang and to which you will return.

If you <u>do</u> need only one word to replace the tired, abused word *God,* simply use the one I am borrowing from your lexicon for this email—WISDOM. It has a certain mysterious ring to it, and yet so earthy, and so available to everyone without distinction.

Or even better, you could simply call me by one of your most familiar names—LIFE—for that is what I AM. Hmmm, *I AM*. I like that one too! I AM LIFE in all its mixture, colors, and shades, visible and invisible—Cosmological Life, Biological Life, Anthropological Life, Sociological Life, Psychological Life, Religious Life—there I go again, borrowing your wonderful human names.

By the way, although it is necessary for me to refer to the pronoun "I" when I am speaking with you, I am not a being nor a larger, older version of you. I am not a he, or a she, or an it. I am an experience—an experience of Life, encountered initially by your body, followed by your mind and your imagination. Body, mind, and imagination are your most important trinity; they are your sacred organs of knowing me, honoring me, and sharing me. Trust not any religion or any religious trinity that denies, devalues, or tries to bypass the human body, because it is your most sensitive instrument to detect my presence. Sadly, its neglect over the centuries has caused much unnecessary suffering, because when your body is denied it causes people to behave badly. Sometimes very badly.

Now regarding emails: Many of you have sent urgent messages in the past few months asking me to intervene in the decisions related to your Supreme Court, your recent elections, and your future elections. Let me say, as an aside, I find that inflated name a little humorous—*SUPREME!?* As the Wisdom of the Universe, I chuckle every time I hear it. Be that as it may, nearly half of your urgent messages want me to intervene in one way, and the other half want me to do the opposite. This is often the case in your urgent messages for my intervention into your human affairs. I am sure that you can see this puts me in a no-win situation. And, again, I don't like to be boxed in as anyone's favorite.

Now let me say clearly, and kindly. This is not my job. It is not my job to clean up the messes of your own making. You made the mess and you need to take the responsibility to clean it up. I am not your parent, neither Father nor Mother, and I am not on call to clean up your rooms. You are no longer children, though it was necessary *once upon a time* for you to frame our relationship that way. Those old images are no longer helpful. Let them go, along with the security blankets and stuffed animals of your childhood.

Clean up your messes using the Wisdom already available within life, within you, and within each other. This includes your bigger messes, like racial and gender inequality, unjust political systems, and wars. I don't need to intervene from the outside. I have been with you from the beginning. I never left and I never will. I do all my work from the inside out, not the outside in. This way we can work together. But you have to do your part.

And while I am on this topic, please stop crediting me with helping you to win ballgames and other sporting events while the losers weep. Or crediting me with helping you to find a parking place at the mall. Or finding the right mate for you on Match.com. It makes me look partial to some and not others, and makes you look kinda childish. So please stop sending those messages. They just fill up my In-box.

Please remember that you have access to all the Wisdom—our common Wisdom—that you need to live creatively and compassionately and to move life along its mysterious unfolding. I know that you keep looking for the doorway to Wisdom outside yourselves in all kinds of places and all kinds of *isms*, including fundamentalism, literalism, rationalism, materialism, and dogmatism. Those doorways will not lead you to the Wisdom we share. They only divide and feed *god-greed*—the illusion that there is not enough of me to go around. I do not know where that fake news started, but please stop spreading it around. It's not true and it has caused too much bloodshed over the years.

The doorway to Wisdom is close at hand. It's an inner doorway. You will locate that Wisdom deep within, underneath your fears and prejudices, and your need to be right and to win at all costs. You are better than that, you are wiser than that, and you are more creative than that. You are more courageous than that. Go into your fears and through them. Just on the other side is that secret passageway. Enter there and you will come to a beautiful meadow out beyond right and wrong, beyond winning and losing, beyond red states and blue states, beyond liberal and conservative, and beyond all the divisions of your making. I will meet you there in that deep inner place. We can converse and decide how to go back into the outer world to create a less conflicted, less terror-filled life together. We need to do so. We must do so. We can do so. You and I working together.

So, carve out time and space in your crowded lives to go within your beautiful, sacred selves to locate the narrow doorway that leads to the beautiful meadow. I will meet you there.

Yours forever,
Wisdom

CHAPTER SIX

BLESSINGS FOR LIFE'S DAILY PILGRIMAGE

The image of life as a mystical path has been nourished by my immersion in the Analytical Psychology of C. G. Jung and by the experiences of leading pilgrimages to places and sites around the world that have been considered sacred. My indebtedness to Jung and his work is well documented throughout these pages. The archetype of pilgrimage has prompted me to lead pilgrimage groups to Ireland, Scotland, India, Machu Picchu, Vietnam, Cambodia, Thailand, and Laos.

Pilgrimage has a long, rich history among those seeking to live a conscious spiritual life. To be a pilgrim, a soul traveler, means to follow in the footsteps of people across all continents and centuries, people who have traveled with spiritual intent and attention. Different from a travel tour, pilgrimage encourages spiritual and/or psychological experience and insight rather than mere sightseeing. A pilgrimage is taken at the urging of soul that hungers for sacred encounter, especially in times of personal or professional transition. In depth psychological language, a pilgrimage facilitates the individuation process.

From a Jungian psychological perspective, pilgrimage may be framed as an intentional desire and practice to expand consciousness in general and religious consciousness in particular. These pilgrimage goals may also be considered the twin goals of the lifelong individuation process described by Jung.

My first pilgrimage 20 years ago took me to Iona, a wee island situated off the western coast of Scotland. A destination for spiritual pilgrims for centuries, Iona was founded by St. Columba in 563 C.E. and became a center for the Celtic spiritual tradition that continues to the present day. With her remote setting, natural beauty, unspoiled body and beaches, and accumulated sacred intent of pilgrims over the centuries, Iona has beckoned me and my pilgrimage groups more than a dozen times. The people with whom I have shared pilgrimages to Iona, and to other remarkable places, remain my primary spiritual community, scattered though we are.

Iona has been one of those temporary homes to which I keep returning, like a mystical homing pigeon or a mystical migrating bird. On Iona, I touch something solid, real, ancient, and ancestral. More importantly, most often I am touched by that something. The holy happens. The sacred suddenly appears in surprising ways, and I no longer feel like a lonely pilgrim, but like a part of a visible and invisible community. I would say that I experience something of soul; not always and not on command, yet surprisingly often.

Iona remains an iconic *thin place* where the metaphorical curtain between the visible/invisible, outer/inner, and conscious/unconscious has been rubbed thin. There is a long-held belief that pilgrimage provides the possibility of participating in the flow of energy between the visible and invisible aspects of the one Ultimate Reality. Carl Jung once suggested that everything we want to learn about psyche/soul can be learned from Nature herself, as analogue. The numinous natural world remains our wisest teacher.

The Celtic image—*thin place*—caught my attention when I first set foot on Iona and has enriched my imagination ever since. *Archetypal Thin Places: Experiencing the Numinosum* became the theme and title of my thesis at the completion of analytical training with The Inter-Regional Society of Jungian Analysts. (See Wright 2018: Chapter Seven, *Thin Places and Thin Times*.)

Over the years, Iona and other pilgrimage destinations have become more than external sacred places. They have become internalized as aspects of soul, as well as *metaphors* for the sacred ground beneath our feet wherever we walk. The primary purpose of making a pilgrimage is to sharpen our awareness that every day and every place is sacred and to enable us to live *as if* that is true.

To that end, the following *Blessings* are some of the ones I composed and offered at breakfast each Iona morning. They were meant to remind myself, and to suggest to others, to *pay attention* to the numinous powers and presences that would predictably emerge through the thin curtain.

They are offered here in the same spirit. May they serve a similar purpose for our daily pilgrimage along a *Mystical Path Less Traveled.*

BLESSINGS

(1)

My Dear Pilgrims,
You are forever springing into my mind
As I await our rendezvous:
Wondering how your own preparation is going
And, more importantly,
How you are <u>being</u> prepared.
Wondering what our alchemy will be,
Individually and collectively.
Wanting so much to manage our pilgrimage well
And wanting even more to trust
The Divine Impulse that enabled us to say "Yes!"
May the stirrings deep within
Move us to bow to the One
Who has charted our path in advance
Who guards our fate
Who desires even more than we

That Meaning be our Companion and Gift.
May the Invisible Pilgrim Guide
Both stir and sooth our souls
And leave no doubt about the value of
Walking a conscious pilgrim path.

(2)

For the safe night's flight
Thanks be to You, Great Pilgrimage Guide.

For the red sunset leaving Newark
"Red sky at night, Sailors' delight."

For the privilege of travel and adventure
And the gift of intent
To travel with wakefulness.

May we sink ever so slowly into that deeper place
Where we know our purpose
And our connection to the All.

Enfold us with your Presence
That we may be fully present to ourselves and others
In the thin moments, places, encounters.

May we remember to bow in gratitude
And to make our willing sacrifices
To open ourselves to all the ways
You desire to meet us during this sacred time:
Through our plans and surprises
In our inspiring thoughts
And moments of despair.

Companion us then
Always nudging us to look deeper
And to move one step below
Where we are at any moment.

(3)

May we know that we are born mystics,
Grounded, Embodied
Attuned to the numinous presences and powers
At the heart of the universe or universes
May we know that we are the stuff of the cosmos
Neither greater than nor lesser than all else
And that all is holy.
May we see ourselves as threshold dwellers
Between the visible and invisible, conscious and unconscious
And from that mysterious intersection
May we live with passion and compassion,
Our twin offerings
For the privilege of our sojourn.
And may we remember to bow seven times a day
Or seventy times seven.

(4)

O Deep Mystery
Who weaves the threads of our little lives
Into something grand
We marvel at your leading and prompting
And ask that we may not shrink
From your stretching.

You who are with us, behind and before
May we now entrust ourselves to this crossing
Our holy destination just over the horizon.

May we attune ourselves to the sacred beat
At the heart of all things
That we may be a part of the rhythm of life
And never contribute to the discord.

As we place our feet on the Holy Isle
May we give ourselves to the experience
Whatever the feeling
Trusting that it is and will be
A part of the sacred alchemy
One further step in the process
Of uniting body and soul, matter and spirit.

(5)

Gathered by Oban's beautiful shore
Awaiting our crossing,
Let us call to mind our long-held expectations
Holding them lightly
Embracing the ancient wisdom
That invites us to
Cast our bread upon the waters
Trusting that it will be returned seven-fold!

(6)

Blessed be the animating Breath
To which we awakened
And the animating Presence
That accompanies all our departures and returns.

Blessed be the longing
Planted deeply within
For the Larger for the More
And the More Meaningful.

Blessed be the combination
Of courage and sacred foolishness
That prompted us to say "Yes"
To the call of pilgrimage
And to the whisper of Iona.

For all the baggage we carry with us
And for that which we left behind
Both gladly and regretfully.
May we lighten our grip
On those things and attitudes
That no longer serve our soul.

May we travel with open eyes
To behold the beauty
Of the visible and the apparent
And may we be attentive to the transparent
That is visible only to the third eye.

As we approach our destination
May we also catch a glimpse
Of our larger destiny
And give our hearts gladly to it.

At the end of this day may we be able to say
"I feasted on the banquet table
That is my one wild, precious life
And I am filled and fulfilled."
May it be so!

(7)

Blessed be the sacred rhythms at the heart of all life
Of day and night, sun and moon
Of ease and dis-ease, delight and dread
Fragmentation and integration
(Life-Death-Resurrection in endless guise).

May we find our rhythm on this sacred soil
Where so many hopeful hearts have come
For so many years.
May we find balance where needed
And disturbance where complacent.

We give thanks for dreams
Both comforting and disturbing
Always offered for soulful balance
Pleading with us to be human
And nothing more.

Here on the edge of the ancient world
May we keep attentive to the edge
That beckons us
And may we take the risk of stepping one foot over
As we continue to walk the Way that leads to Life.

(8)

May the anticipation of the new day
Cause us to quiver with delight.
May the anxiety about the unknown quicken our senses
Yet not close our soul-bodies.
May we not forget the purpose of our efforts
To be with Being itself.

May our third eye be watchful and attentive
To the people and places
We are privileged to encounter.
May our anxieties be transformed into awe
Our tensions into vigilance
Our bodies tuned to befriend
Rather than to flee or defend.
May we trust each step of the path
As much as we trust
That our next breath will be gifted
And the next.
May we trust that all shall be well
And all manner of things shall be well.

(9)

In her poem "I Go Down to the Shore," Mary Oliver, feeling low and miserable, asks despondently, *What shall I do, what should I do?* And the sea says in its lovely voice: *Excuse me, I have work to do* (Oliver 2012: 1).

We, too, have our work to do
On our mystical path
May we like the ocean
So faithful to her rhythms
Be faithful to our natural work
Of becoming more fully ourselves
With all other selves
And when the habitual distractions
That we choose to hide ourselves
From ourselves
(Perhaps an old mood, a discouraging voice,
Lethargy, or mindless busyness)
When those distractions appear on

Our inner shore
May we smile and say kindly
"Yes, I see you … But right now
I have my work to do."
This day's work has never been done before
And will never be repeated
When it is over may we be able to say
It is well, it is well with my soul!

(10)

Blessed be the beautiful body of the Earth
Her body and ours joined as visible partners
And blessed be our invisible partners
Logos and Eros
And their many twin offspring:
Light and Dark, Day and Night
Sun and Moon, Matter and Spirit
Masculine and Feminine
And blessed be the sacred space between them
Thresholds to negotiate again and again
On our daily pilgrimage.
As we walk the mystical path
May we remember the words of Annie Dillard
We are here to witness … that is why I take walks:
To keep an eye on things
May we watch carefully, walk softly, share deeply
And discover anew that all roads
All paths lead to Emmaus
For those who have eyes to see
The image of Christ in all things.

(11)

Continue to resolve, dear ones,
To walk in an expectant, awakened way
Eager to discover the purpose of this day.
All your preparations until now
Have tilled the inner soil
For the seeds and eventual fruits
That await your expectant heart.
Protect then the new life desiring
To be birthed.
Be on guard for the distractions
That are all too eager
To take you away from your best desires.
On the mystical path may you meet
A more ancient, instinctual part of yourself
And may it be a wonderful reunion.

(12)

My soul,
Which is not mine to own or possess
But mine in the sense of being your human voice,
Sound your voice in and through me.
May I trust that you are already sufficient,
That you are wise enough, that you care enough,
That you are the more, and the more, and the never depleted.
May I know in my depths that I, too, am enough
And so are those I meet on the path today.
May we be open to our common soul-life
To allow the mystery of our connection
To add music to the world
Rather than discord.
May I bring to this day

What will be just enough
Rather than what I think will keep me safe
And free from want.
May I keep an uncluttered space within
To which I can return time and again.

(13)

O Deep Mystery
That weaves the threads of our little lives
Into something grand
I marvel at your leading and prompting
And ask that I may not shrink from your stretching.

You who are with me, behind and before,
May I now entrust myself
To this day.

May I stay attuned to the sacred beat
At the heart of all things
That I may be a part of the rhythm of life
And never contribute to its discord.

As I place my feet on the mystical path
That is my life
May I give myself to each experience
Whatever the feeling
Whatever the poles of opposites
Of delight or dread
Trusting that each will be
A part of the sacred alchemy
One further step in the process
Of uniting body and soul, matter and spirit.

(14)

O Divine Wellspring
Source of life and life's end
In whom all the tributaries of life converge,
Take us down the well of our own lives
To the eternal spring within
From which all people, all pilgrims, have drawn.
Water now our thirsty souls
Through story, symbol, poetry, and words we speak,
Through the silences we keep
Through the bread we share
Through all entrusted to our care.
As we draw deeply from the inner Wellspring
May our lives be a wellspring of mercy, justice, and peace.
May it be so!

(15)

(With gratitude to Thomas Merton)

Source and Sustainer of life:
I have no idea where I am going
I do not know the road ahead of me
Or how long
Or when and where it will end
Nor do I really know myself nor the many selves within
Nor do I know the ultimate purpose at the heart of life itself
A purpose far more complex than my mind can embrace
Nor do I know what pleases and promotes that larger Purpose
Yet I think that my *desire* to know
My *desire* to please and promote the Purpose
Does, in fact, please.
On most days, that is enough!

(16)

Sometimes a man, a woman, announces
   he/she is leaving home
      to go on pilgrimage
To leave the daily to and fro
   the come and go
      the sound and fury
To embark on the Great Round
   traversed by millions
      for thousands of years.
They say goodbye to family and friends
   who with envy or skepticism
      wish them farewell and well-being.
They leave the world
   of habit and predictability and order
      to voluntarily upset their routine
Trusting some irresistible, indescribable urge,
   An urge with no audible voice
      yet heard so loudly
         it could not be ignored:
  Go! Risk it! Trust! Get out of here!

May we trust
   that we have been called here to this place
      to this time
         with these familiars and these strangers.
As we give ourselves
   to these precious pregnant moments
Let us strain to hear
   the music from the farther shore
      as we take in the sights and sounds
         of the here, the now,
            the visible, the invisible
               that go before and behind.

(17)

May the hunger and thirst
That invited and drove us here
Be deepened before they are quenched.

May we honor the hunger pangs of our soul
And not be too quick to medicate them
With old remedies and solutions and behaviors
That leave us empty.

May we be given soft eyes to see what is before us
As well as the invisible around and beneath.

May we lean into our dis-ease
And invite it to be our Teacher.

May we seek poverty of mind and heart
So necessary to receive abundance
And embrace the humility of not-knowing
That is part of the gift of being human
Desiring nothing more.

When we come to the end of this day
May we have the satisfaction
Of having shown up and been present
Able to say with passion
"What a gift to be alive
And part of the Great Unfolding!"

(18)

Blessed is the mysterious experience of Being itself
To be here where we can be with other lovely beings

In search of what it means to be
  To be more
    And to be more whole.
For the unquenchable hunger and thirst for meaning
  That goes before us and follows
That inspires us to run like hungry little lambs
  To their mother's utter
    Uttering nothing
      But the swish of thankful tails.
Would that we could be so eager
  With our delight and gratitude
    For our ultimate Source of sustenance.
For the mysterious gift of consciousness
  That grants the capacity to reflect on Nature
    And on the nature of our nature
For memory that makes the past present
  And hope that makes the future seem possible
    We bow.
May we push the edges of our consciousness
  To embrace all that we are
    The good, the bad, the beautiful, the ugly,
And may we show to others
  The same compassionate embrace.
May we use the best of our brain
  In concert with a compassionate heart
    To speak the truth as we experience it
      As we know it
And thus lay an infinitesimal grain of sand
  On the scales of humanity's soul
    To tip it toward life and peace and justice.
Thus, may we live this day to the full
  Since it will never be lived again
    And our days are growing short.

(19)

All bread is holy, sacred, blessed
(With or without magic words)
Because it comes from the Earth, our Mother.
Let us then always eat mindfully, consciously,
Eucharistically
To nourish our bodies
To feed our souls
To nourish our communion
Our common union
With each other
And with all of life.

(20)

These are the sacred, sacramental gifts
Bread from our Great Mother, Earth,
Ordinary food made holy by our gratitude.
May they be visible symbols of invisible Grace
May they feed the Christ-life
That is always growing within you and me
And in all things.

(21)

Sometimes, like this morning, like this moment
My heart overflows with the goodness of life
And life's many possibilities
Like a new poem that sends chills up my spine
And down to the soles of my feet.

Or like the excitement of a new idea
That springs forth from somewhere deep within
And deeper still.

Or like the few hours ahead now of unscheduled time
Lying before me like a blank page
Waiting to be written
Begging for engagement
Not to be used or wasted
But to be lived
Gratefully, expectantly, open-handedly.

Sometimes, like this morning, like this moment,
Heaven and Earth are making love in my bed.

(22)

Blessed be the gift of yet another day
On this holy isle
For the privilege of pilgrimage
While others tend the fires back home
While others seek to bank the fires
Of social and political dis-ease
That demand our daily attention and concern.

We give thanks
For traveling companions
Lovely and soulfully serious
With whom we can risk sharing
Matters of the head and heart
Matters that really matter.

For silent, solitary labyrinthine walks
Resulting in a common tangle
Drawing us ever closer physically and emotionally.

For laughter and hilarity
For getting lost and found
And getting bogged down on sacred ground
(A pretty fair metaphor for us all).

For delicious food
That appears magically
Served by gracious hands
And smiling faces
And for the relief from cooking, washing, cleaning,
And making
Beds.

For this day
A soft one
Covering us like a snug old sweater
Allowing us to sink ever more deeply into ourselves
And into the embrace of the Christ-self.

As we consider the life of Jesus
And those who dare follow his radical way
May we see him and each other
As mirrors
In whom we see aspects of our hidden selves.
May we see the Christ-image
We are invited to incarnate.
May we realize anew that all roads lead to Emmaus
And to a picnic on the beach
Where we, like Peter, are asked
Do you love me?
Do you love me? Do you love me?
If so, feed my sheep
Feed my lambs
Nothing more
Nothing less
May it be so.

(23)

For the irresistible, urgent, and dawning of another day
The irrepressible gift in which to be the gift we are
And shall be
For the divine invitation
To incarnate and manifest the sacred image
In which we were formed
We bow.

For the Invisible Presences that guard this Holy Isle
Presences who have met us at all the thresholds
And allowed our passage
We bow.

For the visible places and people
Who make The Invisible Ones believable
We bow.

For the rhythmic beating of the one Heart
That reverberates through all the world
Just underneath our own skin
We bow.

For time outside time
That helps us to decide how-to live-in time
And to reverence the little time we have
We bow.

(24)

Blessed be our birth and our birthing
Blessed be the union that brought us into being
Blessed be the passion that conceived us

And our passion that continues to co-create
Ourselves, our lives, our world.

May the Beloved who conceived us
Now love us into being beyond
Anything we have yet conceived.

This day as we travel over water and stone
May we glimpse the Strength and Beauty
Of our origins
And our futures.

(25)

Within each of us there is a great ocean.
In the middle of that ocean there is an island.
In the middle of the island there is an altar.
In the middle of that altar
There is a candle
That burns day and night
A candle we did not light
But are invited and tasked
With tending.
Tending that light is our most vital calling
For it is a light that desires to
Shine in and through us.
Let us tend that light with such devotion
So we become the flame
That manifests in our
Passion and *Compassion.*

(26)

Some mornings are so beautiful
That we must shout for all to hear:
WHAT A WONDERFUL DAY TO BE ALIVE!

Every day a new journal page
A new sketch pad
A new poem
A new love to be embodied.

And, yet, if our heart is reluctant to praise
Let it simmer until it is done with its sad stew
For that, too, is food for soul
If sipped consciously.

The Ancient of Days
Will continue its predictable march
Across the cosmic landscape.
Yet we have so few days to spend.
May we spend each wisely, therefore,
Eating, drinking, walking, talking, relating
Mindfully.

(27)

Reading: Old men and women ought to be explorers
Here or there does not matter
We must be still and still moving
Into another intensity
For a further union, a deeper communion.
(T. S. Eliot, *Four Quartets*)

May the spirit of this place
And the spirits of all
Who have made pilgrimage here
Join with our spirits
To continue that further union
That deeper communion
That our Beloved is hosting.
May these final days find us watchful and receptive
To the invisible graces
And the ancient invisible ones
Who walk beside us
And desire our conscious company and conversation.

May these hours be precious in their scarcity
And not a moment wasted on the petty
May our anxiety be transformed into awe
Our hearts filled with gratitude
Our souls filled with wonder
Our bodies blessed with health.

And now may this Eucharistic food
Prepared by invisible hands
And served with smiling faces
Feed our deepest hungers.

(28)

In the stillness, in the silence
Let us simply feel our pulse
Thump-Thump, Thump-Thump
The echo of that first sound
When life burst into being
Our connection to the All
And to all that is.

Thump-Thump, Thump-Thump
Faithful, persistent, called or not called
The heartbeat of the Divine
Ever-present reminder
Of the sacred vessels
We are.

(29)

Blessed be the faithfulness of our small planetary home
As it participates in the fourteen-billion year
Cosmic dance.
And blessed be the invisible hands
That hold the universe together
And move the celestial clock
Without our aid.

We give thanks
For the Ancient Invisible Presences
That we touch with our imagination
That abide just beneath the membrane of our eyelids
Those Abiding Images who accompany us
Encouraging, disturbing, supporting, challenging
Who ask only that we honor them by bowing
Seven times a day
Or seventy.

May *we* companion *them* this day
Even as we pilgrim with each other.

(30)

Eternal Mysteries, the Beginning and the End,
And the In-Between,

Who call us away
And who calls us home/Home
Bless now our little band of pilgrims
So small, so wee, so fragile, so strong
So precious, so full of desire
To be a part of the continuing unfolding
Individually and collectively.

May we look into the eyes of our ending
And see the outlines of our beginning.

Seal into our memory
That which we have experienced
That can continue to feed our soul.

Stretch us this day beyond our comfort zone
Disturb us where we are complacent
Shatter those containers that are too small
To hold sufficient meanings.

May Love continue to transform us
So that we can be a part
Of your continuing, evolving Life.

(31)

As our thoughts turn toward home
Iona asks us her questions:

Are you sad, glad, fulfilled, and desiring more?
Let it be, she says, for all emotions come unbidden
And are purposeful.
Let them simply wash over you, she says,
As the rain washes over my body this morning.

How have I contributed
To your soul's delight, your soul's distress
Your soul's expansion?

Have you found what you came seeking, she inquires?
Did you discover your edge?
Were you able to extend one foot over?

What of your own soul
Did you see mirrored in me, Iona asks?
What did you learn from me about the beauty of Nature?
About the nature of beauty?
About you own beauty?
And will you promise
Never to question that again?

What did you learn about traveling lightly
Through the world?
Will you leave old baggage
That no longer serves your sweet soul?
There is plenty of room here to leave it -
At St. Columba's Bay, Martyr's Bay, and Relig Oran -
For those images of self that diminish your worth,
Attitudes and habits that shrink your soul,
Images of god too small
To house your soul's passion
Too small to embrace all religions
And religious and nonreligious alike.

When you return home
What of me will you long for
And how will you address that longing
And seek to deepen it?

When your family and friends ask you about me,
Iona asks,
What will you say?
What images will you share?

When you return home
Will the ground beneath your feet feel holy?
I hope so, she implores,
For that will mean I have been a good host.
Give my warmest regards, she says,
To the Holy Land where you reside.

(32)

For all the mysteries explored this week - theologically,
philosophically, psychologically - one more mystery catches my
attention this final morning. When the twin lambs are grazing apart
from their mother and all of a sudden charge across the field for her
nourishment, does the urge emerge from within them, or does a
sound, a scent, a *thought* from her beckon them?
From whence does the urge to merge emerge?

Remembering the words of the Monks of Weston Priory, Vermont:
When the time of our particular sunset comes
Our thing, our accomplishment
Won't really matter a great deal.
But the clarity and care
With which we have loved and been loved
Will last forever.

So
May the ties that bind us
And the friendships formed on Iona
Be as solid and strong and beautiful

As her stones
That weigh our pockets
With her lasting gifts
Ready reminders of her soil and soul.
May the images of sheep and lambs
Who taught us, entertained us,
And mirrored our desires
Accompany us home to warm our hearts
As much as their natural coat warms them
Even in rain and wind.
When we count them as a prelude to elusive sleep
May we be transformed back here
To this restful, peaceful place.

May we learn the lessons of wisdom
By counting the scarcity of our days
That we may waste not a moment.

May the memories, the laughter, the music, the tears
Flavor our remaining days
As much as the yummy food
That has graced our tables
Served by graceful hosts.

And may we honor the sighs
Too deep for words
The stirrings too deep to describe
The felt presences and powers
That animate the universe
The invisible Mysteries that
Thankfully
Elude our control and naming.
May it be so!

(33)

Blessed be the wind that carried us to Iona
And swept us across the Holy Isle
Reminding us of the wonderful fierceness
Of the Divine.

Blessed be the wind that softened the last few days
As if to say
"Here is my other face."

Blessed be the wind that is our breath
That sometimes rushes, pants, sighs, gasps, sooths
And always reminds us of our origins.

Blessed be our Homecoming
And the long sigh
Of having made the Great Round.

May the Iona winds continue to blow in and around
On the other side of the Atlantic
To lift us up, to bring us down
To remind us of the Spirit
That ever hovers
And invites us to bow.

(34)

May the Threshold Guardians grant us safe passage
Through all the transitions
And gates on our continuing pilgrimage.

May all the ground on which we walk be sacred
The Promised Land forever sought
And always present.

May the care and intention
With which we loved Iona
And each other
Inform all our living and loving.

May there be nothing ordinary about our lives
But a litany of wonders
To our awakened senses and souls.

Let us remember Rumi's admonition:
People are going back and forth
Across the threshold
Where the two worlds touch.
The door is round and open.
Don't go back to sleep!
(Barks 1995: 36)

(35)

By the authority granted me as your pilgrimage leader
And nearing the completion
Of our visible Iona pilgrimage,
I now declare you to be honorary members of
Numinous Anonymous
And may you never recover
From your addiction to the sacred!

(36)

My first thought this morning turns toward each of you, and I trust
that each is safe, though I am aware that some of you had to cross
surprising thresholds due to flight cancellations.

I went to bed at 9 p.m. and woke at midnight with the following dream image that on first hearing may seem contrived, but not so.

Our pilgrim group is gathered on a beautiful Iona grassy knoll, and I am continuing my leading and teaching. Each of us is "outlined" auralike with a bold, distinctive mark about four inches in width, as if an artist had traced the shape of our whole bodies. I say, "At this place we remember the one Light from which we come, which makes us distinct, which makes us shine."

I awaken, record the image, and for the remainder of the night, in and out of sleep, the final blessing *wrote itself*:

Blessed are we who come from the one Light
That illumines, enlivens, enfolds
And forever shines through us.

Blessed is the light of Iona
That drew us
To her beautiful shores
And fed our souls, our minds, our bodies.

May we now fill in
Incarnate
What we saw in outline and image
Of the Divine
Of ourselves, of our world,

And may we never hide
Our Christ-nature and Light
Under a bushel of fear.

May we have the courage and tenacity
To turn the hunk of stone
(Which is our life)
Into a perpetual poem.

May the memories of Iona
Feed and sustain us
As much as our gracious hotel hosts
And may all our tables be so blessed
With love and laughter.

May we be faithful members
Of Numinous Anonymous
But never recover
From our addiction to the Sacred.

And may we never doubt
That what we experienced on Iona
Was real
And really matters!

EPILOGUE
Final Journal Entry

Journal: (November 6, 2020) I am writing this journal entry on the morning when the states of Georgia and Pennsylvania "turned politically blue," at least for the moment.

It is also the morning after President Donald Trump confirmed to the nation and world what many of us psychological professionals have been saying, and fearing, for the last four to five years. In his 15-minute rant from the White House, he displayed his very fragile, narcissistic, paranoid, psychological structures. We witnessed a psychotic episode by the most powerful leader in the world. He was unhinged. As his carefully crafted, sometimes criminally crafted, political empire was falling around his feet, the walls of his inner empire were collapsing as well.

As I watched, I was terrified, gratified, and relieved. I also felt sad and, surprisingly, I experienced an occasional tinge of empathy and compassion, the reasons for which I mention below.

We can only hope that President Trump can recover enough psychological stability to negotiate the next two months for the health of the nation and world, and for his own family. I hope the same for our nation, and for me.

More personally, I am writing this journal entry two weeks after my own Trump-like psychological eruption. I was talking by telephone with one of my closest lifelong friends. We were simply catching up when she mentioned that she had just voted for Donald Trump for president. Suddenly, I became possessed by some dark inner figure that I am intellectually aware lives in my basement, but now he was fully present! I went berserk, or to use my favorite descriptive phrase, "bat-shit crazy." I told her I was so disappointed in her; that she had been deceived by Trump and Fox News; that she was contributing to the death of our democracy as well as our environment; that she was hurting our children and grandchildren; and that it would be a long time before I could even speak to her again, much less visit her. Yes, I was unhinged!

I was just barely aware that I was being very mean, but I felt justified, self-righteous. Then, knowing how important her Christian faith is to her, I pulled out my most powerful religious weapon. I blurted out, "You can't be a follower of Jesus and a follower of Trump at the same time!" My friend could barely defend herself under my barrage, though she kept offering what I consider Fox News talking points. The conversation lasted about 15 minutes, about the same length of time as President Trump's rant.

For the past four years, I have fielded many questions concerning how to deal with our political differences and how to talk to family members and friends who are "on the other side." And I have been able to provide what I consider to be some helpful suggestions and psychological wisdom. Yet, I failed miserably to follow my own counsel. I made an *F* on the exam.

Following the telephone call, I did not sleep very well or very long. When I woke up, I reached for my journal and wrote for hours. For this final journal entry, I am including some of the raw and the redeeming parts.

Journal: (October 22, 2020) It's the morning after I blasted my friend for voting for Trump. I really went off on her. I was "mean as a snake" or, god forbid, as mean as Trump himself. Last night, I was a monster, one whom I abhor and speak and write against. I find pretty words to tell others, and yet I am the very devil I abhor. Yes, I am both angel and monster! It is one thing to *know god*, and quite another to *know the devil*, and to realize/accept that I channel both; or, as I have been arguing, that I/we *are* both.

There is a great gap, perhaps the widest stretch of all, between knowing what is right, fair, just, and humane and doing/being fair, just, and humane. The greatest sorrow may be the sorrow in knowing what is right, just, and humane and not being able to act on that knowing.

I fear Donald Trump because the monster in him mirrors the monster in me. His monster is totally unleashed; mine is barely contained and broke its leash last night. I am similar to Trump in potential and sometimes in degree.

My fear is deeper than politics, deeper than the election. My fear goes to the very roots of our human being-ness, to our psychological roots, to our capacity, or lack thereof, to choose the angels of good over the monsters of evil. I am afraid. In the words of the great Irish poet William Butler Yeats: *Things fall apart; the center cannot hold / Mere anarchy is loosed upon the world / The blood-dimmed tide is loosed, and everywhere / The ceremony of innocence is drowned / The best lack all conviction, while the worst / Are full of intensity* (Yeats 1977: 184).

(I suddenly remember a journal entry recorded a year ago and I look it up: The world is off its cultural/religious/political axis. We are spinning out of control, and no one has a clue about what to do, really. The center cannot hold because there is no center left. Chaos reigns, and we move from one crisis to the next, buying ourselves to death, collecting stuff, and stuffing ourselves. We are scared shitless or shitting in our pants.)

I am terrified that the divisions and opposites that we have created and that are so visible in numbers in this election, and in the pandemic, may be too great to reconcile. I am afraid that our collective center cannot hold under the weight of the divisions we continue to create. Our collective monsters could well defeat our collective angels—at least in the short term, and maybe for our species.

If Biden wins the election, it may slow our slide toward the proverbial cliff, but only slow it. There is no political solution to our human dilemma and divisions. There is no religious solution as long as our deities and devils remain outside and beyond the human psyche. Nor is there an easy psychological solution. Analytical Psychology can only point us along a healing path, but then we have to walk it individually, consciously, and responsibly. I am afraid for our nation and for our world. We are the victims of our own creating, caught in the *tyranny of tribalism*.

Yet deeper still, after last night, I am afraid that my own center, my own psyche, may break as well. I am afraid that when the chips are down and when I need to access my angels, the monsters may be too powerful. I know so much about how the human psyche works, and doesn't work, yet I doubt that I can deal creatively with what I know.

What if my own psyche breaks under the weight of the opposites? What defenses do I have left? I can no longer call on an external god to intervene, or on Jesus or the Holy Spirit. Who will deliver me from this body of death that I am? The mystical Paul had his answer. What is mine?

Theologically, our deities and devils—our angels and monsters—remain removed at a safe distance. Psychologically, that distance is erased, and at any moment we can, and do, channel both angels and monsters, and sometimes simultaneously. There is a certain safety in theologizing. Perhaps it is necessary until we can reach a level of consciousness to bear the opposites that we are. Religions have provided rituals and symbols to mediate the powers and presences, to *dumb down their power* sufficiently. But when the rituals and symbols have been lost or literalized, all that is left is the *dumb*.

The mystical path, the path of consciousness, requires that we recognize that we carry both angels and monsters in our backpack and suffer the knowledge of the horrible manifestations of the darker side of our being human. We have to look the monsters in the face and see that the face is our own. This is the heaviest of crosses to bear—the cross of our own ambivalence, our inner divisions and opposites—and to suffer those crosses consciously. It is difficult to hang there between the opposites and trust that an unforeseeable third will appear. The emergence of a third may be a good and reliable psychological theory, but when the monsters come calling, all hell can break loose.

The mystical path, the path of consciousness, is less traveled because it is too demanding. It requires too much attention, too much moment-by-moment monitoring of the ever-present angels and monsters. Who wants to live with such awareness? Who can do so? Who would want even to try?

The gate to the mystical path is surely narrow and dangerous, as is the path itself. Who would dare even think about such a path, much less attempt to walk it? Better that we read about it, or applaud those few saints, heroes, and wisdom figures who have chosen to try.

And yet—and yet—it is the only path to real life, to full life. It is the only way out of and through the messes we have created for ourselves.

And yet—and yet—it really is the only path available for us humans because the path, as well as the angels and monsters, is in our DNA. We are they. We carry our angels and monsters consciously, responsibly, or we give them to someone else to carry for us.

I must telephone my friend and retrieve my monsters that I visited upon her last night. I will tell her how sorry I am about my words and behavior. I will apologize and ask for her forgiveness. I will tell her that I am very afraid. I will tell her it frightens me that Trump and his allies have been able to deceive so many people, including those I love dearly, like her and her family.

I will tell her that what frightens me more, however, is that I can sometimes be as mean and as hurtful and as much of an asshole as Trump is most of the time. And last night was one of those times. I will tell her that I have no excuse for my terrible, fearful rant and that I am sorry that she was on the receiving end. I will tell her —contrary to my declaration last night that I do not want to talk to her or to visit her ever again—I would like to see her more often and soon, and I will call her again in a couple of days to check on her.

And that is what happened.

My journal entry for that morning concluded with the following:

I am out there
Naked before the Cosmos
The Great Mystery
With neither god-shield
Nor religion-shield
For protection.

All has been stripped away
Or tossed aside
And I await the consequences of
Living religiously naked.

There is no going back
Nor can I see ahead
I stand vulnerable
Awaiting lightening
Or enlightenment
Or both
Or neither.

My consolation is the strange freedom
That comes with knowing
That I am naked and defenseless
And that I house my Redeemer
If there is one
Who is taking its own good time
To appear
Lost as it seems to be
In the labyrinth
Of my own inner contradictions.

I may run out of time
Before the Helper appears
And if so
May my gravestone read:
He made his pilgrimage
He cast his lot
He made his bet
Never sure if he won or lost
But convinced he could do no other.

SOURCES CITED

Barks, Coleman. (1997) "The Breeze at Dawn," *The Essential Rumi*, Edison, NJ: Castle Books.

----(2006) "The Guest House," *A Year with Rumi*, New York, NY: HarperCollins Publishers.

Barrows Anita and Macy Joanna. (Trans). (1996) *Rilke's Book of Hours: Love Poems to God*, New York, NY: Riverhead Books.

Browning, Elizabeth Barrett. (1992) "Seventh Book," *Aurora Leigh*, Chicago, IL: Chicago Review Press. (Original work published in 1856).

Dourley, J. (2010) *On Behalf of the Mystical Fool: Jung on the Religious Situation*, New York, NY: Routledge.

---- (2014) *Jung and His Mystics*, New York, NY: Routledge.

Edinger, Edward F. (1996) *The New God-Image*, Asheville, NC: Chiron.

Hollis, James (2013) *Hauntings: Dispelling the Ghosts Who Run Our Lives*, Asheville, NC: Chiron.

Jaffe, Aniela. (1989) *Was C. G. Jung a Mystic?*, Einsiedeln, Switzerland: Daimon Verlag.

Jung, C. G. (1916) "General Aspects of Dream Psychology," *The Structure and Dynamics of the Psyche, Collected Works, Volume 8*, Princeton, NJ: Princeton University Press.

---- (1924) "The Spiritual Problem of Modern Man," *Civilization in Transition, Collected Works, Volume 10*, Princeton, NJ: Princeton University Press.

---- (1927) "Mind and Earth," *Civilization and Transition, Collected Works, Volume 10*, Princeton, NJ: Princeton University Press.

---- (1935) "The Tavistock Lectures," *The Symbolic Life, Collected Works, Volume 18*, Princeton, NJ: Princeton University Press.

---- (1946) "On the Nature of the Psyche," *The Structure and Dynamics of the Psyche, Collected Works, Volume 8*, Princeton, NJ: Princeton University Press.

---- (1952) "Answer to Job," *Psychology and Religion: West and East, Collected Works, Volume 11*, Princeton, NJ: Princeton University Press.

---- (1953) "Individual Dream Symbolism in Relation to Alchemy," *Psychology and Alchemy, Collected Works, Volume 12*, Princeton, NJ: Princeton University Press.

---- (1957) "Commentary on the Secret of the Golden Flower," *Alchemical Studies, Collected Works, Volume 12*, Princeton, NJ: Princeton University Press.

---- (1958a) "Jung and Religious Belief," *The Symbolic Life, Collected Works, Volume 18*, Princeton, NJ: Princeton University Press.

---- (1958b) "Epilogue to Jung," *The Symbolic Life, Collected Works, Volume 18*, Princeton, NJ: Princeton University Press.

---- (1959) "Christ, A Symbol of the Self," *Aion, Collected Works, Volume 9ii*, Princeton, NJ: Princeton University Press.

---- (1960) Letter to M. Leonard, 5 December 1959, in G. Adler and A. Jaffe (eds) *C. G. Jung Letters, Volume II, 1951-1961*, Princeton, NJ: Princeton University Press.

---- (1965) *Memories, Dreams, Reflections*, A. Jaffe (ed), New York, NY: Vintage, Random House.

---- (1973) Letter to P. W. Martin, 20 August 1945, in G. Adler and A. Jaffe (eds) *C. G. Jung Letters, Volume I, 1906-1950*, Princeton, NJ: Princeton University Press.

---- (1977) *C. G. Jung Speaking*, W. McGuire and R.F.C. Hull (eds), Princeton, NJ: Princeton University Press.

Lachman, G. (2010) *Jung the Mystic*, New York, NY: Penguin Books.

Newell, John P. (2011) *A New Harmony*, San Francisco, CA: Jossey-Bass.

Oliver, Mary. (1992) "The Summer Day," *New and Selected Poems*, Boston, MA: Beacon Press.

---- (2012) "I Go Down to the Shore," *A Thousand Mornings,* New York: Penguin Press.

Sabini, Meredith. (ed). (2002) *The Earth Has A Soul,* Berkeley, CA: North Atlantic Books.

Schweizer, Andreas and Schweizer-Vüllers, Regina. (eds). (2017) *Stone by Stone,* Verlag, Einsiedeln: Daimon.

Stein, Murray. (2017) *Outside Inside and All Around,* Asheville, NC: Chiron.

Tippett, K. (2020) "On Being." Radio Podcast, Episode 869, Minneapolis, MN.

Yeats, W. B. (1977) "The Second Coming," *The Collected Poems of W. B. Yeats,* New York, NY: MacMillan Publishing Company.

Wright, Jerry. (2018) *Reimagining God and Religion: Essays for the Psychologically Minded,* Asheville, NC: Chiron.

Zeller, Max. (1975) *The Dream, The Vision of the Night,* Boston, MA: Sigo Press.

CPSIA information can be obtained
at www.ICGtesting.com
Printed in the USA
FSHW011408040321
79140FS